Cookie Stories

Cookie Stories

Life Stories and the Cookies that Inspired Them

By Penny McConnell and Kathy Sutton

Illustrations by Gretchen Reed

Falling Star Press
Austin, Texas

Falling Star Press
P.O. Box 10628, Austin, Texas 78766
(v) 512-458-4363
(f) 512-458-8618
www.fallingstarpress.com

"The Cookie Thief," page 86, copyright by Valerie Cox. Originally published in *A 3rd Serving of Chicken Soup for the Soul*. Reprinted by permission of the author.

ISBN 0-9769026-0-5

Library of Congress Control Number: 2005927522

Printed in the United States of America. First Printing 2005

Quantity discounts are available on bulk purchases of this book for gift purposes or as premiums. For information, please contact the publisher, Falling Star Press, P.O. Box 10628, Austin, Texas 78766. Telephone 512-458-4363.

Cover illustration by Gretchen Reed
Book design by Chris Thiele
Photo of authors by Laura Vassberg

To Louise and Nancy, our moms.

You inspire us every day. Your love has been a lifelong blessing.

Table of Contents

Introduction 1

Notes on Cookie Baking 4

Romance 5

Passion 25

Family 47

Sharing 75

Holidays 99

Cookie Wisdom .125

Ask Penny 133

Index to Recipes 142

Share Your Story 143

About the Authors 144

Acknowledgements

OUR LIST

To all of our *Cookie Stories* contributors, thanks for taking the time to share your personal stories with us. We couldn't have had a book without you!

Thanks, Jean, for testing and organizing our recipes, doing research, and believing in our success from the very beginning.

Destiny, you're so impressive. You're the best intern anyone could ever have! Thank you for your time and effort and the care you gave to *Cookie Stories* and to us. Mozart's isn't the same without you. We miss you!

Lisa, thanks for volunteering your time to facilitate our *Cookie Stories* focus group (and for being our cheerleader in so many other ways!).

Renee, Katrina, Robena, Evelyn, Diane, Leslie, Margaret, Lisa, Alicia, Marika, Julie, and Pam ... a great group of women who we treasure and appreciate. Thank you for showing up and for giving us your time, ideas, suggestions, and creativity.

Cassandra, Joia, Brenda, Robyn, and Diane. Thanks for always being there for both fun and panic. We appreciate that you always made time for an "emergency" book group when we needed it!

Rusty and Laura, thanks for allowing us to take your normally quiet space and interrupt the calm with laughter and giggles as we wrote the pages of *Cookie Stories*. Thanks, too, for the sparkling water, green tea, and cheddar Goldfish. When you said "help yourself," you probably didn't realize we would take you seriously!

Gretchen, thanks for making our words come alive with your illustrations. It's been fun working with you. The fat woman with the banana and the wolf dog captured us from day one. Really!

And finally, George. Thank you for being the editor, publisher, counselor, voice of reason, task master, and member of our *Cookie Stories* team. We sincerely thank you for your contribution and genius. How many times did you say, "You don't have to worry about that, you don't have a book yet." Look, George, we have a book!

KATHY'S LIST

Zachary and Alex. May you come to love Snickerdoodles as much as your Dad, Uncle Dennis, and me. Ask Mimi to make them for you sometime.

Bryan, Cynthia, Dennis, and Tami. You're the best support group a

Acknowledgements (continued)

girl could have. Thanks for always being interested in the latest *Cookie Stories* update. I love you.

Wilbur and Jupiter. I appreciate your loyalty and contribution to my life. Your warm greeting after long *Cookie Stories* meetings was always so welcome!

PENNY'S LIST

To my customers, employees, and supporters. It's been my pleasure serving you, working with you, laughing with you, and learning from you.

To Ginger, my childhood baking buddy. You've made a loving contribution to both my life and my company.

Cookie, the richness of our phone calls! You've probably listened to half the manuscript of *Cookie Stories* by phone. Thanks for your humor, your unwavering support, and your loving heart.

Beth, you're always there for my next big idea or project. We'll always have Savannah, and remember, I love you more.

To my cute little Potato Heads, Morgan, Jordan, and Tascha. You're the sweetest kids on the planet. Mom loves you.

Solomon, you are my unfolding treasure, and I love you without reservation. Thanks for sharing me with Kathy for the past two years.

Introduction

Kathy is tall, with shocking blue eyes, long blond hair, single, and in her middle thirties.

I am shorter, divorced, with twin adult boys, dark skin, big brown eyes, and in my (very!) early fifties.

Most days I go to work at Penny's Pastries, my beloved cookie bakery, in shorts and a T-shirt covered by a "vintage" sweat shirt. On the other hand, Kathy cruises to work in a convertible sports car to her demanding, high-powered human resources job.

And we've been girlfriends for more than ten years. Of course we can talk by phone for hours. Or meet at book group, local festivals, movies, and makeup counters. The night *Cookie Stories* was born we were sitting in a booth at Mangia Pizza in Austin, Texas, drinking icy cold beer and sharing a deep-dish pizza. As we both reached for a second helping, I shared a sweet story about an event that had happened during my work day.

I was at Food!Food!, one of my cookie accounts, when I noticed a mom buying her little boy a Penny's decorated cookie. She handed her son the cookie while she took care of the payment. As she waited for her change, she looked down at her son and asked him if he liked the cookie. The cute four-year-old looked up at her and replied simply, "My tongue is smiling."

Kathy loved the little story and excitedly said, "You know, we should write a book. I bet there are lots of people out there with great cookie stories." She said this in the same way she'd spontaneously say, "Let's take a road trip" or "Let's plan a party."

And over the next two years in many ways it felt like a party. Within weeks of the book idea, we ran all over town putting up flyers in coffeehouses, restaurants, and sandwich shops, inviting people to submit their personal cookie stories. We used email, personal phone calls, and quick, hand-written notes to our friends, clients, and contacts requesting that they send us their stories.

We were both delighted with the response. We read stories, submitted from every part of the country, written by both men and women, of every ethnicity and generation. Sometimes we giggled at the stories, and sometimes they were a little sad. But as we read, we remembered our own personal cookie stories and our sessions lasted for hours as we talked, typed, and shared. Over weekend cups of cappuccino or late lunches on sunny patios all over Austin, *Cookie Stories*

developed into pages of shared memories, intimate connections, and a wonderful validation of the importance of family and friendships.

The stories, along with our personal thoughts, seemed to naturally fall into six cookie categories. You'll read about romance, passion (and passion that sometimes crosses the line into obsession), family, cookie connections, holiday memories, and cookie wisdom. At the beginning of each section you'll be invited into our ongoing conversations as we created the manuscript. In addition, *Cookie Stories* gives you almost two dozen cookie recipes from my bakery and great baking tips for making cookies in your home kitchen.

Cookie Stories is truly a labor of love for both Kathy and me. It's ultimately about the tiny details and the dramatic events that make up all of our lives. It's about shared human experiences that lead us back time and again to the profound importance and the joy we find in our friends, our families, our partners, and our communities.

Through the pages of *Cookie Stories*, it is our sincere hope that you'll make the connection and remember your own cookie story.

Notes on Cookie Baking

Your kitchen probably contains most of the equipment you'll need for an afternoon of cookie baking. Supermarkets and restaurant supply stores can supply the rest. Here are a few suggestions for ensuring professional-level results.

Baking sheets. There are several types on the market, however, heavy-gauge aluminum pans measuring 12" x 17" that have edges about an inch high work extremely well. They are sometimes called jellyroll pans.

Decorating supplies. From pastry bags, to professional paste colors, to tips and couplers. If you're just starting to enjoy the experience of decorating cookies at home, a trip to a decorating supply store will pay off.

Parchment paper. Also known as pan liners, all cookie recipes in *Cookie Stories* will ask that you first line a cookie sheet with parchment paper. Available in supermarkets or cake decorating stores, usually in rolls that resemble waxed paper, parchment paper will allow you to bake cookies without using an oil spray.

Portion-control scoops. Professional portion scoops (also known as ice cream scoops) are great to have in your home kitchen. Available in sizes from tiny to extra-large, they are perfect for scooping cookie dough. By using scoops, your cookie balls will go in the oven a uniform size, bake evenly, and produce finished cookies that look professionally made.

Wire racks. As soon as your cookies are cool enough to hold their shape, transfer them from the baking sheet to a wire rack to finish cooling.

Romance

It's All in the Timing

k Penny, when is the perfect time to make cookies for a man?

p Well, I think it's all in the timing. Women like to bake cookies for a new man because it's a "sweet" thing to do, but some of the things we call "sweet" can actually backfire if we do them too early in a relationship, don't you agree?

k You're right. Seems like showing up at his doorstep the day after your first date loaded down with a tray of freshly baked cookies and sweet bread could scream "commitment" to some men and actually scare them off.

p It's a mistake we women make—doing that too early in a relationship. There was a time in my life when I could find myself in a full-blown relationship over a pastry and a cup of coffee!

k We've all been there, haven't we? "I think I like him a lot so let me whip up a batch of home-style brownies." Never understanding that we could inadvertently remind him of his mother and end the relationship before it even has a chance to begin!

If you don't count the occasional movie, concert, or dinner date, or the flurry of dating activity I experienced in those heady days after the pain of my divorce faded, I have had very few important men in my life. On the other hand, Kathy, not yet married, has had quite a few boyfriends in the period of time that I've known her. So we're very different when it comes to numbers, but we are in concert when our discussions turn to men and timing.

Based on personal experiences and countless hours of conversation, the Law of Relationships handed down in the book of Kathy and Penny says that relationship success or failure is all in the timing. Returning his telephone call, answering his email, sweetly whispering "yes," or baking that first batch of cookies—all must be executed with the timing of an air traffic controller if you want the relationship to have wings.

For most people, kids, parents, grandparents, and girlfriends, baking a batch of cookies is viewed as a simple act of appreciation that doesn't require a list of timing instructions. They'll appreciate the effort and reward us with warm little smiles and kisses.

Men, on the other hand, are wonderful but complex. When a woman presents a man with a plate of homemade cookies early in the relationship, something happens. That plate of cookies turns into a symbol of something big and momentous. We may not understand this, but we must respect it. Go ahead and bake cookies, but watch the relationship's temperature or you could get burned.

For instance, my sister Cookie (yes, that's her lifelong nickname!) knew a man who had moved from our frigid Midwest hometown to Dallas, Texas. She thought he might still have some potential in her life so she came up with this cookie idea that, on the surface, seemed inspired. She asked me to bake and decorate several dozen cookies with a winter theme—snowmen, caps, mittens, and Christmas trees—for him. Of course the objective of all this decorating was to remind him of what he was missing—a white Christmas … and her. We shipped the box along with her handwritten note. She didn't hear from him. When several weeks had passed she called him and was greeted with a very formal voice, thanking her for the cookies and little else. She told me he was simply overwhelmed and a little frightened by her cookie effort. Kathy and I would say it's just another example of bad timing!

However, if a man makes cookies for a woman, it feels different, doesn't it? He's gone into the kitchen and taken out a recipe book that probably hasn't been used in years. It means he's interested. If everything else is in place then it's all very charming. Instead of the commitment panic a man might feel, we award him a few brownie points for his effort.

The question remains—when is the perfect time to make cookies for a man? We've determined that after a few casual dates is certainly not the time. But what a difference a few months can make. When a commitment has been made nothing is more appreciated than baking a batch of his favorite cookies. Suddenly it means what cookies always represent—caring and value.

The Best of Intentions *as told by Jean Louis*

When I was a sophomore in college I met a guy, let's call him Les. He seemed like a nice, normal guy. We went on a date and had a really nice time. I thought we were clicking. The next Sunday I was feeling domestic and decided to bake some cookies. I made chocolate chip cookies and brownies. Since I made much more than I needed to eat myself, I decided to deliver a plate of cookies and brownies to Les. I called and asked if he minded if I dropped by for a little while, and he seemed excited I was coming over. But when he opened the door and saw the cookies, he looked totally shocked. He freaked out. He said I was moving way too fast and he wasn't ready for a commitment. I was just bringing him cookies, but he saw a minister and a baby carriage. He never called again and I never made cookies for a casual boyfriend again.

Jean may have had timing issues with this guy, but now she spends her life with her wonderful husband, six children (ages 2 to 28), six grandchildren, and three beagles. Jean offers no rules to live by when it comes to cookies, but prefers them soft, chewy, and warm with a tall glass of cold milk. Creative at heart, she has launched her own photography business specializing in portraits of children in natural light.

A Cookie Date *as told by Brett Bishop*

Fifteen can be an awkward age for anyone. Combine a lack of self-confidence with absolutely no dating experience and you can end up with one terrified teenager. Add a few cookies in the mix and you end up with a high school cookie story.

I had a very good friend at school named Donita. I had known her all through junior high school, and we had managed to keep in touch during high school. Somewhere along the way she transformed into the most beautiful girl I knew. I couldn't believe this was the same person that I used to kid around with in class and had considered to be just one of the guys. Discovering how attracted I was to her interfered with my basic life functions such as breathing, talking, and thinking.

Three rules govern Brett when it comes to his cookies—he eats only the ones he likes, no dunking (he takes them straight), and chocolate chip cookies are good anytime, anywhere. Making his living as an engineering manager, Brett dreams of being able someday to support his lifestyle by working as a full-time writer.

We had talked on the phone a bit, but never anything serious. I had no idea how to ask her out on a date. Something as simple as, "Would you like to go out and do something sometime?" never even entered my mind. But I knew I wanted to see her.

Donita knew my mother was sick and had been away in the hospital for some time. I was describing the situation at home with Mom out of the house, and I could sense that Donita was genuinely concerned. My mind, all hopped up on hormones, slammed into overdrive. This was it! I saw an opening and knew this was the moment I had been patiently awaiting. I told Donita that my mother was coming home in the next couple of days (completely true) and I had wanted to bake some cookies for her return (mostly true). But I claimed I didn't know how to bake cookies and needed someone to help me with the recipe (a complete lie).

That night I played movies in my head. Donita would come over and we would bake cookies. We would get playful in the kitchen and at some point, I would grab her by the waist and pull her close to me. We would embrace for a long moment, smile gently, and then run off into the night—the beach, Vegas, some deserted island; I didn't really care where we went as long as we were together. I may have gotten three hours of sleep that night but it was all worth it as I imagined the wonderful journey on which I was about to embark.

The next day Donita arrived right after school like she said she would. I turned the oven on preheat, and she did the rest. She mixed the batter and spooned out the cookies onto the cookie sheet. Then she put them in the oven. She looked so beautiful. Then just when I thought our romantic moment had arrived, she washed her hands in the sink and told me that I could take the cookies out of the oven in about 15 minutes. She dried her hands, said good-bye, and was out the door before I knew what had happened.

I never attempted to ask her out on a date after that, but then again, Napoleon never returned to Waterloo. She had done exactly what I had asked her to do under the pretense of doing a good deed. She was a wonderfully sweet girl and I can only imagine what may have been if I had only told her what I really wanted.

A Gesture of Love *as told by Brenda Harrison*

Every day for the length of her marriage, my grandmother (whom we called Mama Ruth) made four freshly baked chocolate chip cookies for my grandfather. She served him two cookies during his noon meal and two after his supper. Unbelievably she did this for the nearly 50 years they were married. The bowl of cookie dough was always there, and when my brother and I would visit, Mama Ruth would allow us to scoop a big spoonful of this fantastic stuff right out of the red Pyrex bowl. Later, after I grew up and married, I was able to fully realize the sweetness of her gesture. When I look back on the tradition Mama Ruth created, I better understand the preciousness of this gift to my grandfather.

Brenda is a woman who lives by her own rules. While most people say they love warm, fresh-from-the-oven cookies, Brenda prefers her favorite oatmeal walnut cookies cold and crispy from the refrigerator. Most would say never substitute cookies for a wholesome meal; Brenda says they're great as an occasional meal replacement! Happily married, this free-thinker loves jobs with movement and variety and credits raising her five children and climbing the Aztec pyramids in Mexico City as her biggest life events.

Penny Suggests: Romantic Cookies

When the timing is right there's nothing better than a warm plate of cookies to set a romantic mood. Close your eyes for a minute and imagine a cold winter's night. Okay, let's go all the way and add a storm or snowfall to this scene. But inside it's warm and cozy. (Is there a fire blazing in the fireplace?) With thick blankets on the floor and mugs of hot cocoa you add a plate of freshly baked cookies. You're talking, laughing, nibbling, there's melting chocolate—you get the picture.

Black Magic/White Diamonds

Dark, deep, sultry cookies that have an almost brownie-like middle. They may give you significant spread when they bake, however, so don't crowd too many on your baking sheet.

Yield: 4 dozen cookies
Temperature: 325 degrees
Baking Time: 10-12 minutes

INGREDIENTS

3 cups semisweet chocolate chips (divide in half)

¾ cup (2¼ sticks) salted butter, softened

5 ounces unsweetened baking chocolate

5 large eggs

2¼ cups granulated sugar

1½ cups all-purpose flour

1 teaspoon baking powder

⅛ teaspoon salt

2 cups nut meal*

1¼ cups walnuts, chopped

1½ cups white chocolate chips

* Nut meal can be purchased at specialty food stores, or you can make it at home. See "Ask Penny" for directions.

DIRECTIONS

1. In a small saucepan over low heat, melt 1½ cups of the semisweet chocolate chips with butter and unsweetened chocolate. Watch closely so as not to burn the mixture. When smooth, remove the mixture from heat.

2. In a separate bowl, combine flour, baking powder, salt, and nut meal. Set aside.

3. Pour melted chocolate into an electric mixer bowl. Add eggs and granulated sugar. Mix on low speed until thoroughly combined.

4. Add dry ingredients to mixer bowl. Combine all ingredients until batter is formed and no white streaks of flour remain. Fold in the chopped walnuts. The finished cookie dough will seem slightly soft.

5. Divide the finished dough into two bowls. In one bowl add the remaining 1½ cups semisweet chocolate chips. In the other bowl add the white chocolate chips.

6. Cover the bowls with plastic wrap and set the dough to rest and firm up in the refrigerator for approximately one hour.

7. Preheat the oven to 325 degrees. Line cookie sheets with kitchen parchment.

8. Scoop the refrigerated dough (using an ice cream scoop or tablespoon) onto prepared cookie sheets. Leave room for the cookies to spread by placing just nine cookie balls on each sheet.

9. Bake for 10-12 minutes, rotating the pans once during the baking cycle. When the cookies are ready to remove from the oven, the outside edges will be completely set and the middle will be cracked and slightly soft. Make sure not to overbake. Allow the cookies to cool for a few minutes before removing them from the pan.

Chocolate Chip Indulgence

This classic combination of brown-sugar cookie dough baked with big splotches of melting chocolate brings out the unbridled passion in all of us. Our recipe calls for loads of chocolate chips, pure extracts, and a secret ingredient—nut meal (from walnuts, pecans, or even almonds). The meal along with the thick dark corn syrup adds tenderness and moisture to the finished cookies. Yum!

Yield: 3-4 dozen cookies
Temperature: 325 degrees
Baking Time: 12-13 minutes

INGREDIENTS

3 cups all-purpose flour

1/4 cup nut meal*

1 teaspoon baking soda

1 teaspoon salt

2 large eggs

1/2 cup dark corn syrup

1 tablespoon pure vanilla extract

1 tablespoon whole milk

1/2 cup (one stick) unsalted butter, softened

1/4 cup vegetable shortening

1/2 cup granulated sugar

1 cup light or dark brown sugar, firmly packed

2 cups semisweet chocolate chips

* Nut meal can be purchased at specialty food stores, or you can make it at home. See "Ask Penny" for directions.

DIRECTIONS

1. Preheat oven to 325 degrees. Prepare cookie sheets with kitchen parchment.

2. In a large bowl, combine flour, nut meal, baking soda, and salt. Set aside. In a smaller bowl, combine eggs, corn syrup, vanilla, and milk. Set aside.

3. In an electric mixer bowl using a low speed, cream butter, vegetable shortening, granulated sugar, and brown sugar until creamy. With mixer still running, add liquid ingredients to the creamed mixture. Mix until thoroughly combined.

4. Add dry ingredients to the mixer all at once. Mix on low speed until blended and cookie dough is formed. Turn off mixer and add chocolate chips using a wooden spoon.

5. Using an ice cream scoop or tablespoon, portion cookies and place them on prepared cookie sheets approximately one inch apart.

6. Bake cookies 12-13 minutes, rotating the pan once during the baking cycle.

7. Transfer to a wire rack to cool.

👄 Ginger Brownies

Serve this spicy, mysterious brownie to your partner and you'll get (and keep) his attention. Finish it with the brown-sugar glaze and serve it in small squares. Wonderful with plump, cool strawberries.

Yield: 1 13" x 9" pan
Temperature: 325 degrees
Baking Time: 35 minutes

INGREDIENTS

1 cup (2 sticks) salted butter, softened

4 cups light or dark brown sugar, firmly packed

4 large eggs

1 teaspoon pure vanilla extract

3 cups all-purpose flour

1 teaspoon salt

1 tablespoon ground ginger

1 1/2 tablespoons baking powder

1 cup chopped pecans

GLAZE

1 1/2 tablespoons salted butter

2 1/2 tablespoons light or dark brown sugar, firmly packed

2 1/2 tablespoons whole milk

1/4 to 1/2 teaspoon pure vanilla extract

1 cup sifted powdered sugar

DIRECTIONS

1. Preheat oven to 325 degrees. Line 13" x 9" pan with foil and spray with nonstick cooking spray. Set aside.

2. In an electric mixer bowl, mix the butter with the brown sugar. Add eggs and vanilla and combine.

3. In a separate bowl, combine the flour, salt, ginger, and baking powder.

4. Add the dry ingredients to the creamed mixture and process until batter forms.

5. Fold in the chopped pecans.

6. Spoon brownie batter into prepared pan. Batter will resemble thick cake batter. Smooth the top with a wet rubber spatula.

7. Brownie will bake a total of 35 minutes. Midway during the baking cycle, remove pan from the oven and gently tap it on the work surface, making the brownie fall. This will give the finished brownies a chewy texture. Return pan to the oven and finish out the baking cycle. The finished brownie will be golden brown, completely set along the outside edges and slightly soft in the middle.

8. Remove from the oven, and prepare the glaze.

GLAZE

1. In the pot of a double boiler or in the microwave, melt the butter, brown sugar, and milk. Add the vanilla.

2. While still warm, pour the mixture into the bowl of an electric mixer. With the mixer on low, slowly add the sifted powdered sugar. The glaze should be rather thin; it will thicken as it cools.

3. Spread the glaze over the brownies. Before cutting them into squares, make sure the glaze is set and the brownies are completely cool.

Cowboy Cookies

When it comes to "connecting" with men, these cookies are like a secret weapon. Every man on the planet loves Cowboy Cookies. My partner, Solomon, doesn't really eat sweets, except Cowboy Cookies. I always keep some in the freezer for him. He'll pop two or three cookies into the microwave and devour the whole lot while standing in the kitchen.

Yield: 3 dozen cookies
Temperature: 325 degrees
Baking Time: 10-12 minutes

INGREDIENTS

3 cups all-purpose flour

1 1/2 teaspoons baking soda

1/8 teaspoon salt

1/2 cup (1 stick) salted butter

3/4 cup shortening

1 1/2 tablespoons honey

1 1/2 cups light or dark brown sugar, firmly packed

1/2 cup granulated sugar

2 large eggs

1 tablespoon pure vanilla extract

4 cups old-fashioned rolled oats (not instant)

1 1/2 cups shredded coconut

1 1/4 cups toffee pieces

DIRECTIONS

1. Preheat oven to 325 degrees. Line cookie sheets with kitchen parchment.

2. In a large mixing bowl combine flour, baking soda, and salt. Set aside.

3. In bowl of an electric mixer, cream butter, shortening, both sugars, and honey on low speed until smooth. Add eggs and vanilla to the creamed mixture and process until combined.

4. Add flour mixture to creamed mixture. Process until a soft dough forms.

5. Add oatmeal and process on low speed until incorporated. The dough will be heavy. Add coconut and toffee pieces and combine.

6. Using an ice cream scoop or tablespoon (rounded), place cookies one inch apart on prepared cookie sheets. For a bigger cookie, flatten the dough.

7. Bake 10-12 minutes, rotating pans once during the baking cycle. The finished cookies will be puffy and golden brown.

8. Transfer to wire rack to cool.

Passion

Operating from Passion

k Penny, do you have a personal definition for passion?

p I say we're born passionate and passion is something we can bring "to" any activity. What do you think?

k I agree that passion is internal. I just wish I could tap into it all the time. Of course every once in a while that feeling can cross over and I have moments of "obsession" too!

p Yes, no question about it. We're all familiar with obsession. From the "I can't believe I ate the whole thing" issue …

k … to "I'm obsessed about this guy" and can't quit driving by his house to see if his car is in the garage! Luckily we're able to rein it in most times without causing too much drama.

p You? Me? Drama?

I come from a long line of big, loud, laugh-till-you cry people. My mother is the queen of the laugh. I have an old picture of her that I simply adore. She's holding my tiny twin boys, one cradled in each arm, her head thrown back with her mouth opened wide, eyes shining with delight. I can hear her laugh, throaty and infectious. My twin boys, along with every other member of my family, can find something funny in every simple life event. More times than I'd like to remember I had to go to my boys' teachers and explain that this "inappropriate laughter" problem is something they come by naturally.

Kathy and I also laugh a lot together. Believe me, with Kathy's wonderful sense of humor she'd fit right into my family.

The truth is that nothing makes me feel better and more authentic than a good laugh. I think it's one reason I love working in a bakery kitchen. Commercial kitchens are full of passionate people who talk trash, love openly, drink too much, dance spontaneously in the middle of the kitchen, eat like it's the last supper, and laugh loudly and often. Working late into the night with these wonderful people, music blaring over the constant hum of big, hot ovens and mixers flapping cookie dough, have been some of the best times in my life.

I wish I had a videotape of the year we serviced a national airline with cookies for its in-flight service. We'd gone from a small, three-employee shop scooping cookies by hand to a 10,000-square-foot facility with over 30 employees producing more than 40,000 cookies a night. Fraught with production, distribution, labor, and forecasting problems before the first cookies came out of our ovens, Penny's Pastries crackled with chaos. Even though the work was hard, hot, and steady, my people made it feel like a New Year's Eve party celebrated in chocolate-stained aprons and tight jeans. In truth I was facing the biggest challenge of my professional life; nothing compared to the consequences if we failed. And we failed. Big time.

I've been asked many times how I made it through those bad times and where I developed the personal resolve to rebuild my company. I made it through because of my passion for the work. I made it through because those people encouraged me to never lose my spirit, my drive, or my ability to have a good, soul-deep laugh regardless of the situation. I am forever grateful

to my employees. When I look back at that challenging time, between every layer of disappointment, personal failure, and pain, there is love, possibility, creativity, and God-given passion.

However, if you've ever felt the glow of personal passion like I have, there's a chance you've also been introduced to its darker side—obsession.

I have to admit that more than a little obsession has dotted my life, usually around a relationship gone bad. Haven't we all left more than one message on an answering machine? I have to admit to driving halfway across town in the middle of the night just to check out a dark parking lot to see if his car was there. It's as if some powerful emotion has gripped me and I've crossed over to the "dark side." This happens in the kitchen, too.

For instance, our quality control at Penny's is fairly simple: follow the formula carefully, then take a little bite of the finished cookie. If it ranks near the top on the delicious scale, you've done your job well. More often than not, I'll take that bite and leave the rest of the cookie for someone else to finish. But every once in a while I'll start with a tiny taste, declare it perfect and think I'm done—until I hear that voice in my head calling me to take another bite. Before I know what hit me, I'm involved in a flurry of cookie-eating activity!

The Land of Plenty *as told by Michelle Goodwin*

My roommate volunteered to bring dessert to a potluck at church. Her small faith group consisted of only ten people, so making chocolate chip cookies seemed like a good choice. While she was baking them the aroma filled the entire house. I said to her, "You aren't going to be so cruel as to not let me have one of those cookies, are you?"

She said, "No problem. There's plenty. I'm making two dozen. The next batch I'll take some out for us to eat while they're still warm." So with some cookies on the cooling rack and six already in a cookie tin waiting to be sealed, I was served three cookies hot from the oven.

We didn't even move from the kitchen. "Oh, these are so good," I said, putting the last morsel of melted chocolate in my mouth.

"They really are," she said. "Do you want another one?"

Michelle is clear when it comes to cookies. She likes her cookies big, full of chocolate chunks, still warm from the oven. She's been known to say, "Never be afraid to use more chocolate in your cookies. It's the sign of a brave woman." A Catholic campus minister at the University of Oklahoma, Michelle has traveled extensively and dreams of one day writing books while living in a beach bungalow.

"Really?"

"Sure, there's plenty."

"Okay," I said, and we each had another one. She left the kitchen to let the rest of the cookies cool and to change clothes for the potluck. I sat down in the living room to watch TV. At the first commercial break I decided I wanted something more to eat, so I went into the kitchen. There were the cookies; she won't miss two more, I thought. So I took two more, rearranged the cookies on the cooling rack so it wouldn't look so sparse, and settled back in the living room to watch my program.

My roommate came out of her room dressed and ready to go to the potluck. As she made her way into the kitchen she announced, "I think I'll have one more before I leave." I smiled as she passed by. Then, I could hear her counting the cookies as she put them in the cookie tin.

"Michelle?" she called.

"Yes?"

"How many cookies did you eat?"

"I don't know. Why?" I asked, getting up from the couch.

"There are only 12 cookies left; there are 10 people in the group, and this is the dessert for the meal. What am I going to do?" she asked, looking at me with the open cookie tin in her hand.

Silence. Then I said, "Well, we could eat one cookie each, then you will have 10 and everyone will get one." She laughed, and then added, "Or, I could go to the grocery and get a different dessert."

"You could do that," I said.

"Cookie?" she asked, offering me some from the tin.

"I'll just take one. Thanks."

No, Thank You *as told by Arlie Skory*

When we were growing up we lived with two cookie extremes: the wonderful cookies and the awful cookies. The wonderful cookies were my mother's sour cream twists. Whenever she made them, we had to divide up the cookies so each of us got our fair share. These cookies were hoarded and carefully guarded. The awful cookies were the store-bought windmill cookies. We hated them, but Mom had a rule that applied to cookies and cereal and other kid food: no new cookies (or cereal or whatever) until the old cookies were used up. Therefore we'd eat the windmill cookies just to make them go away.

Our extreme feelings about these cookies can be summed up in a story about my younger brother. Our family was camping with a number of other families at a northern Michigan state park. My brother, who was nine or 10 years old at the time, decided to go exploring on his own. Although we were

Arlie's high school sweetheart and husband of 28 years knows she has one rule when it comes to cookies—if you want one, go get your own. She may not be willing to share her cookies, but she generously shares her life with him and their 20-year-old adopted daughter from Korea. On cold winter days in her hometown of Lansing, Michigan, you'll find Arlie curled up in a comfortable chair with a cup of Earl Grey tea, a good book, and a generous plate of her mom's sour cream twists.

allowed to ride bikes in the campground, he went outside the park and got lost in the woods on the other side of the highway. His abandoned bike was found by a gravel pit. We frantically searched for him for hours to no avail.

Meanwhile, he had walked away from the gravel pit in the wrong direction and had come out on a different highway. Fortunately he was picked up by a nice family who saw him at the side of the expressway and stopped to help. They knew he was hungry so they offered him the only food they had in the car—windmill cookies!

As my brother tells it, that was just the final straw. Being lost for hours in the woods and coming out on an expressway was bad enough, but being offered windmill cookies broke his reserve and brought him to tears!

Penny Suggests: Passionate Cookies

If there's a single ingredient that makes both cookies and life grand, it's got to be passion. Kathy and I come to it from different angles. I simply believe I am a passionate person and bring it to everything I do, every conversation I have. On the other hand, our on-the-move Kathy fills her life with wonderful events, people, and experiences that create a passionate lifestyle. In the end, the journey to passion isn't important. Whatever your personal style, just love it, be it, live it.

Razza Ma Taz

One of the most passionate bakers of all time is my sister Ginger. An inspired, life-long baker, she created most of the gourmet brownie recipes for Penny's Pastries, reaching her crowning point with this one. It's simply over-the-top decadent.

Yield: 1 13" x 9" pan
Temperature: 325 degrees
Baking Time: 40-45 minutes

INGREDIENTS

6 ounces unsweetened baking chocolate

3/4 cup (1 1/2 sticks) salted butter

1 1/2 cups all-purpose flour

3/4 teaspoon baking powder

2 1/2 cups granulated sugar

5 large eggs

1 tablespoon pure vanilla extract

2 cups raspberry jam, seeded or unseeded

3/4 cup semisweet chocolate chips

3/4 cup pecan pieces

FINISH

1/4 cup raspberry jam, seeded or unseeded

1/2 cup white chocolate chips

DIRECTIONS

1. Preheat oven to 325 degrees. Line 13" x 9" pan with foil and spray with non-stick cooking spray. Set aside.

2. Over low heat, melt baking chocolate and butter in a saucepan or in the top of a double boiler (or in the microwave). Set aside and let cool.

3. In a separate bowl, mix the flour with the baking powder and set aside.

4. With an electric mixer, combine sugar with eggs and vanilla until smooth. With the mixer still running, add melted chocolate and butter in a steady stream.

5. Turn the mixer off and add flour mixture all at once. Process until smooth and all flour streaks have disappeared.

6. Add 2 cups of raspberry jam to the batter. With the mixer on low speed, process until combined.

7. Fold semisweet chocolate chips and pecan pieces into batter.

8. Pour batter into prepared pan and smooth the top with a wet rubber spatula.

9. Bake 40-45 minutes, rotating brownie once during the baking cycle. The brownie is ready to come out of the oven when the sides are completely set and the center is slightly soft. Place the brownie (still in the pan) on a cooling rack.

FINISH

1. Over low heat, melt the white chocolate in a saucepan or in the top of a double boiler (or in the microwave). Watch closely to make sure it doesn't burn.

2. Melt the reserved $1/4$ cup raspberry jam in the microwave just until the jam is melted and warm.

3. Using a pastry brush, brush a thin layer of the melted jam over the surface of the warm brownie to give it a shine.

4. Dip the tines of a fork into the melted white chocolate. Using a flick of the wrist, drizzle melted chocolate over the surface of the brownie in a random pattern.

5. Let the brownie cool completely before cutting.

✒ River City Apricot

This is Kathy's passion. Every time she savors the buttery shortbread base and the thick apricot filling she turns to me and says (like she's never said it before), "I LOVE this cookie!" Note: If your personal passion is a simpler cookie, just prepare the cookie base for River City Apricot and roll and cut the dough with your favorite cookie cutters. You'll be rewarded with tender, melt-in-your mouth shortbread cookies.

Yield: 3 dozen cookies
Temperature: 325 degrees
Baking Time: 10-12 minutes

INGREDIENTS

1½ cups (3 sticks) plus 1 tablespoon salted butter
1½ cups powdered sugar
3¼–3½ cups all-purpose flour*

FILLING

1 18-ounce jar apricot preserves
2 tablespoons cornstarch

*If you are using a heavy mixer with a paddle attachment, use 3½ cups of flour. If you are using a hand-held or rotary mixer, use 3¼ cups of flour.

DIRECTIONS

1. Preheat oven to 325 degrees. Line cookie sheets with kitchen parchment.

2. In an electric mixer bowl, process butter with powdered sugar until completely incorporated and smooth.

3. Gradually add flour to the creamed mixture. Process the ingredients on low speed until a heavy dough forms. Set aside.

4. In a small bowl combine apricot preserves with cornstarch. Mix until cornstarch has been completely and thoroughly combined with preserves.

5. To prepare cookies: Scoop cookie dough using either an ice cream scoop or a tablespoon. If you use the tablespoon, roll the portion of dough in your hands to form smooth balls. Place the scoops or balls of dough onto prepared cookie sheets. Using the backside of the scoop or tablespoon, press into the dough balls to create a deep well to hold the apricot preserves. Make sure you don't press so hard that you break the bottom of the cookies.

6. Using a teaspoon or pastry bag, fill the wells half-full with apricot preserves. Do not overfill.

7. Bake cookies 10-12 minutes in hot oven, rotating once during the baking cycle.

8. Watch the cookies closely, especially in the last few minutes of the baking cycle. When the preserves are bubbly, remove them from the oven. The finished cookies will be very light in color, not golden brown.

9. Transfer to a wire rack to allow the cookies to cool and the jam to set before enjoying.

Chubbie Chunky

With its sublime texture and generous use of cashews, every luscious bite of this dark chocolate brownie is a memorable experience. No need for additional adornments here, just bake it up, let it cool, and cut.

Yield: 1 13" x 9" pan
Temperature: 325 degrees
Baking Time: 25-30 minutes

INGREDIENTS

1 cup all-purpose flour

$1/2$ teaspoon baking powder

$1/2$ cup (1 stick) salted butter

4 ounces unsweetened chocolate

2 cups granulated sugar

3 large eggs

1 teaspoon pure vanilla extract

$1/2$ cup chopped salted cashews

$1/2$ cup semisweet chocolate chips

$1/2$ cup dark raisins

DIRECTIONS

1. Preheat oven to 325 degrees. Line 13" x 9" pan with foil and spray with non-stick cooking spray. Set aside.

2. In a small bowl, mix flour with baking powder and set aside.

3. In a medium saucepan over low heat, melt butter. Remove from the heat. Add baking chocolate and stir until it melts.

4. Add the sugar to the saucepan, stirring until blended. Then add eggs and vanilla, blending completely.

5. Add the flour mixture to the chocolate mixture. Blend completely until all flour streaks disappear.

6. Fold in the nuts, semisweet chocolate chips, and raisins.

7. Spoon batter into prepared baking pan. Smooth the top with a wet rubber spatula.

8. Bake for 25 to 30 minutes, rotating pan once during the baking cycle. The brownie is done when the sides are completely set and a toothpick inserted one inch from the sides comes out slightly coated.

9. Let the brownie cool and cut into squares.

Peanut Butter Obsession

Lee, my first real boyfriend after the divorce, couldn't get enough of peanut butter cookies. I had just started Penny's Pastries when he finally persuaded me to add his favorite cookie to our collection. I made special batches for him, which he adored. For a short while life was grand with Lee, the cookies, and me. And then it started to crumble. It got to the place that if he had to decide between a plate of cookies or me, the cookies would have won. Needless to say he is now an ex-boyfriend, but I got a fantastic recipe out of the deal.

Yield: 4-5 dozen cookies
Temperature: 325 degrees
Baking Time: 12-14 minutes

INGREDIENTS

$4\frac{3}{4}$ cups all-purpose flour

$1\frac{1}{2}$ teaspoons baking soda

$\frac{3}{4}$ teaspoon salt

1 cup (2 sticks) plus 2 tablespoons salted butter

1 cup light or dark brown sugar, firmly packed

$1\frac{3}{4}$ cups granulated sugar

$1\frac{3}{4}$ cups extra chunky peanut butter

3 large eggs

1 tablespoon pure vanilla extract

$1\frac{1}{4}$ cups semisweet chocolate chips (optional)

DIRECTIONS

1. Preheat oven to 325 degrees. Line cookie sheets with parchment.

2. Combine flour, baking soda, and salt. Set aside.

3. In electric mixer bowl, cream butter with both sugars to combine. Add peanut butter and incorporate.

4. Add eggs and vanilla to mixing bowl and process, scraping the bottom of the bowl to make sure mixture is integrated.

5. Add the flour mixture to the creamed mixture just until all flour is incorporated. You will have fairly heavy dough. If you'd like, add chocolate chips.

6. To prepare cookies for baking, take approximately one rounded tablespoon of cookie dough in your hands. Make a ball of the dough and place on the cookie sheet. Repeat until you have filled the sheet, placing the cookies approximately one inch apart to allow for spreading. Press the cookie balls with your fingertips or, if you prefer a more traditional look, use the tines of a fork.

7. Bake 12-14 minutes until golden brown, rotating the pan once during the baking cycle.

8. Transfer to wire rack to cool.

Family

When the Smell of Cookies Feels Like a Hug

k You know, Penny, I remember growing up a happy, contented child with a great family. But I have to tell you, when I was four years old, I ran away from home.

p Oh, my gosh! Did you take the time to pack a bag? What were you so upset about?

k Mom remembers me packing a small bag. I really don't know what I was upset about, but even the thought I might miss Santa's visit wasn't enough to keep me home.

p Gee, you had to be very upset to be willing to miss the fun of Christmas morning. However, at four I'm assuming you didn't make it very far.

k Well, I made it as far as a family friend's house in the apartment complex. She gave me cookies and milk to calm me down, and we talked a while. By the time my mom came to get me, the crisis had passed and I was more than ready to go home.

p Moms seem to be good at so many things. Like ending a crisis and bringing life back to normal. And then, of course when we get older they do that advice thing really well.

I walked into the local Chili's restaurant and immediately spotted them. An attractive mom and her honey-blonde daughters. In the middle of the table sat the quintessential Texas snack food—spicy salsa, surrounded by crispy tortilla chips and ice-cold sodas. As I approached the table, I heard their easy laughter and chatter. I was there because a wedding was being planned and Penny's Pastries would provide the wedding favors. As I slid into the booth, I was starting to feel that familiar tingle of party-planning excitement. What I couldn't have predicted was that somewhere in the middle of the consultation I would be brought to tears.

I'd first seen Kasi (the bride) and her Mom (Tammy Blue) out of the corner of my eye at the autumn Bridal Extravaganza where Penny's Pastries was a first-time exhibitor. We'd worked on our new wedding collection for months before the event, but the morning of the show I was nail-biting nervous. I knew our cookies were beautiful, but I feared the thousands of brides who were expected to visit the show would simply not "get it." In the comfort of my own bakery, the cookies seemed fun, creative, and special. But what would they think? I wanted "oohs and aahs" followed by genuine interest. I feared I'd instead get blank stares, polite smiles, and that sympathetic look that says you've spent far too long in your own isolated little world. Well, as the doors opened and literally thousands of brides flooded the aisles, I heard the excited squeals of women as they spotted the cookies. End of nail-biting, we were a hit, and I was in heaven. In the middle of all this activity I spotted Kasi and her mom as they fingered our sample cookies and cookie place cards. Their initial excitement turned into a formal bridal consultation booked at Chili's.

Kasi, simply glowing with youth and optimism, was to have an early evening wedding at a beautiful venue in Austin. Her maid of honor was her 14-year-old sister, Tolva, and over two hundred people were expected to help the couple celebrate their love. As Kasi and I chatted and started the process of picking just the right cookies, Kasi turned time and again to her mom to ask her advice. As the cookie order was set and the consultation was nearing its natural end, Kasi and her attendants went to use the powder room, leaving Tammy and me to wrap it up and finish our sodas. Somehow in that moment our casual conversation turned to the importance of our children and the kind of life she wanted for her girls. I added that I wanted the same for my boys as they made their own decisions that took them away from me and into the world. Suddenly my eyes caught Tammy's misty eyes and without warning I, too, felt that indescribable feeling of love for children and family—followed by watery eyes and a lump in my throat. As the girls returned, Tammy and I gave each other a little hug and said our good-byes. I left with a smile in my heart. It was just the most feel-good afternoon.

Sometimes when I listen to the evening news or read the newspaper, it seems as if the values of the American family are fading. That parents spend more time thinking about and planning careers than nurturing their families. That children can generally be found holed up in their bedrooms pointing and clicking.

We're told that kitchens go unused, children unheard, and grandparents uninvolved.

Yet, every day, I experience something completely different. Through Penny's Pastries it has been my pleasure to help literally thousands of people plan special events for those they love. My experience says the American family is still alive and well. Yes, parents may be busier with jobs and extra duties, but at the core, their care and love for children, spouses, and community is ever present. I've tenderly pinched the cheeks of tiny babies as we've planned the pastel cookie trays to celebrate first baptisms, helped a roomful of 10-year-old boys and girls plan a good-bye party for a favorite teacher, and cried at wedding consultations. In my world, we still leave cookies for Santa and send kids off on their first day of kindergarten with a big, yellow school bus cookie tucked in their lunchbox along with a handwritten note from Mom.

Magic Cookies *as told by Paulette Moore*

Chocolate chip cookies have always been a tradition at our home and even though all my sons are married with their own families, they still expect chocolate chip cookies when they arrive home for a visit. Little did I realize that cookies are magical, able to soothe and reassure even the loneliest of grandchildren!

In April 2001, Tony, my oldest son, and his family decided to move from Austin, Texas, to Evansville, Indiana, to live near me. They were to live with me in my home until they found a place of their own, and what a joy it was to have them with me. A month after their arrival, Aundra, my daughter-in-law, wanted to return to Texas for the wedding of her youngest brother. It was too soon for the entire family to return, so the plan was for Aundra to fly there for four days and leave Tony and the grandchildren with me. I knew this would be quite an experience for them, especially for Monet,

A devoted mother, grandmother, and social worker, Paulette (otherwise known as Granny) Moore has been working with homeless women and children for about 20 years. She enjoys cooking for her family and being at family gatherings with all of her children and grandchildren. And, of course these events would not be complete without plates of soft, chocolate chip cookies.

the almost-3-year-old, who wasn't quite sure about this move to strange Indiana! She also did not like separations from her mother, even with Daddy there.

The first two days went fine; however, by the time the third day came Monet was getting very lonely and scared that Mom would not return, and things began to fall apart. Even a trip to see Arthur, the cartoon character, and a ride on the mall merry-go-round brought only temporary relief. What could I do to help her through this? As my mind raced for things to do, I remembered baking cookies and how much my children enjoyed them. That was the answer!

"Oh, Monet," I called, "how would you like to help Granny bake cookies—and not just any cookies, but 'magic cookies!'" She was excited, and wanted to know what magic cookies were. "Well," I said, "I will show you, but first we have to learn the magic cookies cheer and then go to the store for ingredients." She was ready with her bright eyes and curious mind to learn the cheer. It went like this, I told her: "Two bits, four bits, six bits, a dollar, we love magic cookies, so this is how we holler!" Then we would yell as loud as we could. It was all she needed! We proceeded to the store with Tony driving, and Monet and I yelling our cheer. Once inside we proceeded to the dairy section and picked up the bag of ready-to-bake "Magic Cookies!" We returned home, and twenty minutes later, we ate cookies and yelled out our cheer. A new tradition had begun, and the magic of it lasted until her mother returned the next day.

The secret to magic cookies is getting them done as quickly as you can, because little girls can't wait, grannies sometimes get tired after three days of baby-sitting, and the joy of baking cookies is not always how you do it as much as who you do it with!

Cookies for Sale *as told by Troy Nalls*

My cookie story takes me back to my hometown of Long Beach, California, where my family always seemed to be the first in the neighborhood with the cutting-edge technology or newest gadget available. For instance, we were the first to have a VCR and the first to have cable television.

However, in 1976 there was one piece of technology that changed my life and put me on my lifelong quest as an entrepreneur. It was a big, brown Magnavox microwave oven. I remember there were no settings on the microwave except HOT. It had one big knob that was the timer, but if you were not careful it could reduce a meal to an unappetizing blob within seconds. Be that as it may, the neighborhood kids were captivated. They marveled at how you could take a bowl of cold food and have it hot in less than a minute.

This gregarious guy and lifelong cookie consumer now spends his days setting up communication systems for small and medium-sized businesses in Austin, Texas. A self-proclaimed family man, Troy is married and is the proud father of three children. His favorite cookie is oatmeal raisin (but he won't turn down chocolate chip with macadamia nuts), and he enjoys soaking them (not dunking, but soaking) in milk while he sits in his favorite chair watching sports events on television.

One day while experimenting with this new toy, I discovered that if you set the timer just right it could turn a hard store-bought cookie into a soft chewy cookie. (This was in the days before groceries sold soft-baked cookies.) I was so excited that I invited my buddies over to try my new soft cookies. Soon the word got out, and kids of all ages and some adults were knocking at my door at all hours to try MY cookies!

In a flash, my business idea was launched. At Mr. Green's store just around the corner from our house, you could buy a package of 20 stale no-name cookies for 50 cents a bag. One day I stopped by after school and bought two packages of the chocolate chip cookies using my lunch money. I wish I could still remember the exact date of this purchase because it was truly the day I started down the path of making my living through my own small business. I dreamed my cookie venture would make people happy and supply me with enough extra money to play Asteroids and support my growing candy habit.

I set up shop selling four cookies for $.25. I could usually sell about two complete packages of cookies per day. What I did not know then was that I had a product with a generous profit margin and no overhead. (Gee, I miss the good old days!)

This new venture went on for about four months without a hitch. Then I received the devastating news that Mr. Green had put in a microwave to heat up sandwiches and other fast foods—for free. It goes without saying that my business went from thriving to dying in less than a week.

I must say the cookie business was not only fun but taught me three valuable lessons that are still useful in my business 25 years later: timing is everything, take advantage of an opportunity while the window is open, and word of mouth is indeed very powerful.

But probably the bottom line is that a hot chocolate chip cookie works every time to help you win friends and influence people.

# Rainy Days...and Cookies? *as told by Cookie Barnes*

I love to have cookies when it is raining and I am on the inside, toasty warm, and looking out. This is truly a throwback to my childhood. On these days I am reminded of a wonderful housekeeper and babysitter my mother hired to take care of my three sisters and me.

Mrs. Dixon was one of the "sisters" from the church we attended. She was an elderly, grandmotherly lady; quite proper. She always wore an apron and spent most of her time in the kitchen, with the four of us closely beside her. When Mom wasn't at home she filled the bill, quite well, as a surrogate.

As I said, Mrs. Dixon was proper, that is until storm clouds formed and thunder began to rumble. Mrs. Dixon, you see, was superstitious and believed that "God was about to have His way"—and she had no desire to stand in His way.

A fan of Penny's Pastries since its inception (she's Penny's sister, after all), Cookie describes herself as a cookie "gulper" (not "dunker") with coffee or milk on the side. Her only rule when eating cookies? "I only eat one serving at a time. That doesn't mean the whole bag won't be eaten in a single day, it just means I eat it one serving at a time." Born and raised in Michigan, Cookie says the best time to eat cookies is right after the first snowfall, in a warm house, when cookies are fresh from the oven. Her motto? "Everyone should take the time to find enjoyment in something so simple as a cookie."

On these days she would call us, "Come in the house, quickly." But unlike most children called from play, we were not angry. We knew something very special was in store, for on those days when the sun went behind the clouds and the sky grew dark, Mrs. Dixon would call us into the kitchen and we would make gingerbread cookies!

We would roll out the dough and cut the wonderful shapes of little men, some small, some large; first one eye and then the other, a big smiling mouth; a drizzle of black or golden yellow for hair; don't forget the socks and shoes. (I always liked to do mine in black so that they looked like patent leather!)

By the time the rain had actually appeared and all the lights were out (because, according to Mrs. Dixon, "It's dangerous to leave electricity on in a storm") we would sit at our old gray-and-red Formica-topped and chromed table, watching the rain beat against the window, drinking "silver tea" and eating gingerbread men, by candlelight. I love rainy days and cookies.

# Grandma C *as told by Phil Borror*

(In memory of Mary N. Coldiron, 1900–2000)

The day of Grandma C's funeral was bright and sunny and the two-hour drive to the small southern Ohio town allowed ample time for the required crash course in family genealogy. Review the names of aunts, uncles, and children and how they connect to the family; and the births, deaths, marriages, and divorces that you would be expected to discuss during the day's events.

It seems appropriate that small-town funeral homes were once stately residences now turned into the parlors where we sit surrounded by wallpapered walls outlined with thick wood trim to bid loved ones good-bye. Quiet time spent

Phil, a father, husband, sales manager (for more than 35 years), and lifelong cookie lover, has taken on a new mission in life—to spoil his newborn granddaughter. Can it ever be too early to teach someone to love oatmeal walnut cookies with a frosty glass of milk? A funny man, he says the best cookies are like his grandkids—sweet and full of goodness. When he's not at his demanding daytime job or babysitting his granddaughter, he likes to play golf, scuba dive, or work in the yard. Phil dedicates this cookie story to his mother-in-law, Mary Hilscher, daughter of Grandma C (the best grandmother ever).

remembering how her house always smelled of lilac perfume, how she always carefully folded and saved the empty bread wrappers once the loaf was gone, and how her eyes sparkled when you came to visit.

The service proceeded sedately, and then the eulogy was given by a distant nephew whose connection with Grandma C happened to be overlooked during my tutoring session. He began to recount his memories of Grandma when he had been stationed in Vietnam and how she had always found the time to regularly send him her special batch of oatmeal raisin cookies along with newspaper clippings and news of those at home. Those letters and her cookies brought so much of the warmth of home and made the time spent in such a terrible place bearable. His friends raved about how good the cookies were, and he told how there always seemed to be more guys stopping by his tent after mail call than any other time.

Upon completion of his tour of duty he had stopped by Grandma C's house to thank her for the mail and the cookies and asked her for the recipe for her now famous oatmeal raisin cookies. Throughout the years, he recounted in the eulogy, he had tried many times to bake those cookies, paying strict attention to the recipe, but with little success. At first he assumed that he was measuring the ingredients wrong; or perhaps, he decided, it had been the loneliness of being so far from home that had given them that special taste. But, he told us, it was only as he looked for one last time at that wonderful lady's face, that he realized she had left out of the recipe the most important ingredient, one not available in any store. That special ingredient: a generous scoop of Grandma C's love.

Mom's Homemade Cookies *as told by Rhonda Cloos*

My mother's homemade cookies were a special part of my childhood. I can still hear her voice, "Here Rhonda, have a cookie," as she handed over one of her buttery rounds. Her chocolate chip cookies made our house the place to gather after school, and her sour-cream Valentine cookies were in high demand when they showed up in my college dorm. Wherever they appeared, Mom's cookies were gone in a jiffy.

Sadly, my mother was gone all too soon. She died in 1977 when I was just 23. Today, my mother's talent lives on through her recipes. The cookies allow my children an opportunity to sample her specialties, but there's another treat in store every time I whip up a batch. The recipes—in Mom's beautiful, curvy handwriting—are written on the backs of receipts, calendars, and other paper scraps. One recipe is a clear statement of how times have changed: it is on the back of a television repair bill for 78 cents! Without intending to do so, my mom preserved both her recipes and a peek at the '50s and '60s.

Rhonda Cloos, originally from Chicago, comes from a long line of cookie lovers. A busy freelance writer in Austin, Texas, she carves out time to bake cookies for her children. She has defined a careful strategy for eating cookies (If the cookie is round, eat all around the outside and then go for the middle!) yet to her children's chagrin she feels you should never eat more than two cookies at a time!

Penny Suggests: Comfort Cookies

There is simply this wonderful, tender connection between cookies, childhood, and family. As a child, I baked cookies with my sister Ginger, then shared them with my other two sisters, Beth and Cookie. I continued the tradition with my boys, Morgan and Jordan. Kathy warmly remembers connecting with her mom over batches of cinnamon-dusted Snickerdoodles as an after-school treat when she was a little girl. Actually, she also remembers tuna casserole with fondness, but that's another story.

 # Snickerdoodles

This is similar to the recipe Kathy's mom made. Her recipe had its origins in a cookbook she received as a wedding present 40 years ago. Over the years the cookies became the family favorite, always to the delight of Kathy, her twin brother Bryan, and younger brother Dennis. Kathy's mom says she looks forward to the day when Zachary and Alex, her two grandchildren, can join her in the kitchen.

Yield: 5 dozen cookies
Temperature: 350 degrees
Baking Time: 8-10 minutes

INGREDIENTS

1 cup vegetable shortening
1½ cups granulated sugar
2 large eggs
1 teaspoon pure vanilla extract
2¾ cups all-purpose flour
2 teaspoons cream of tartar
1 teaspoon baking soda
¼ teaspoon salt
3 tablespoons granulated sugar
3 teaspoons ground cinnamon

DIRECTIONS

1. Preheat the oven to 350 degrees. Line cookie sheets with parchment.

2. In an electric mixer bowl, mix shortening with 1½ cups granulated sugar. Mix thoroughly, but do not overmix.

3. In a separate bowl, mix eggs with vanilla. Add to creamed ingredients and mix until combined.

4. Blend flour with cream of tartar, soda, and salt. With mixer running on low speed, add dry ingredients to the liquid ingredients and process until cookie dough forms.

5. Mix remaining sugar and cinnamon together in a small bowl.

6. Shape dough into 1-inch balls and roll in the cinnamon sugar. Place 2 inches apart on prepared cookie sheets.

7. Bake 8-10 minutes, rotating pans once during baking cycle. Transfer to a rack to cool. These cookies puff in the oven, but flatten and turn rather chewy as they cool.

Molasses Cookies

My friend and exercise buddy Robena asks for these cookies all the time. They're really just a good old-fashioned cookie with a lot of spunk. Kids love them too. Wonderful with a mug of hot cocoa.

Yield: 3-4 dozen cookies
Temperature: 350 degrees
Baking Time: 12-15 minutes

INGREDIENTS

$1\frac{1}{2}$ cups vegetable shortening

$2\frac{1}{4}$ cups light or dark brown sugar, firmly packed

2 large eggs

$\frac{1}{4}$ cup molasses

5 cups all-purpose flour

4 teaspoons baking soda

$\frac{1}{2}$ teaspoon salt

1 teaspoon ground cloves

2 teaspoons cinnamon

2 teaspoons ground ginger

Additional granulated sugar for dipping

DIRECTIONS

1. Preheat oven to 350 degrees. Line cookie sheets with parchment.

2. In electric mixer bowl, cream vegetable shortening with brown sugar. Add eggs and molasses to the creamed mixture and process until completely combined, watching not to overmix.

3. In separate bowl, mix flour with baking soda, salt, and all spices. Add dry ingredients to creamed ingredients. Process the ingredients until a cookie dough forms. If the dough seems soft, pop it in the refrigerator for an hour for the dough to rest and firm up.

4. In a small bowl, pour about a cup of granulated sugar.

5. Using your hands, roll pieces of dough into 1-inch balls. Coat the cookie balls with the granulated sugar and place on the prepared cookie sheets an inch apart.

6. When all the sugar-dipped cookie balls are on the cookie sheets, dip your fingers in water and lightly sprinkle the water over the balls of dough. This gives the cookies their traditional crackly finish.

7. Bake 12-15 minutes, rotating pan once during the baking cycle. Repeat with remaining dough.

8. Transfer to a wire rack to cool.

Grandmother Lewis' Tea Cakes

This recipe comes from one of my customers, LeeAnn. Several years ago we baked tons of these cookies for her daughter's wedding reception. LeeAnn declared that the Penny's-baked tea cakes were a wonderful tribute to her Grandmother Lewis. As a seventh-generation Texan she shares the recipe with love of family and Texas pride.

Yield: 4 dozen cookies
Temperature: 325 degrees
Baking Time: 10-12 minutes

INGREDIENTS

1 cup (2 sticks) salted butter

2 cups granulated sugar

3 large eggs

½ cup buttermilk

4 cups all-purpose flour, sifted

1 teaspoon baking soda

2 teaspoons pure vanilla extract OR

2 teaspoons nutmeg

DIRECTIONS

1. In a small bowl sift flour with baking soda (and nutmeg, if you use it). Set aside.

2. In electric mixer, cream butter with sugar until smooth. Add eggs and buttermilk (and vanilla, if you use it) to creamed mixture. Process until thoroughly blended.

3. Add dry ingredients to liquid mixture to form cookie dough.

4. Remove dough from the mixer bowl and pat into a rectangle. Cover with plastic wrap and chill for several hours or until firm.

5. Preheat oven to 325 degrees. Prepare cookie sheets with parchment.

6. Dust rolling surface and rolling pin with flour. Roll dough to a $1/4$-inch thickness and use your favorite cookie cutter or a simple round biscuit cutter to form cookies. Place them on the prepared cookie pan.

7. Bake until golden brown, 10-12 minutes, rotating pan once during the baking cycle.

8. Transfer to a wire rack to cool.

# Butterscotch Chews

If I were ever asked the "deserted island question" I would answer, without hesitation: my mascara (and maybe just a little blush), pictures of my family, books, and a generous tin of these cookies. If you think you don't like coconut, let that go. In this cookie, you'll love the finished combination. Perfect for sharing or giving as a gift in a pretty tin.

Yield: 3-4 dozen cookies
Temperature: 325 degrees
Baking Time: 11-13 minutes

INGREDIENTS

3 cups all-purpose flour

1¼ teaspoons baking soda

1¼ teaspoons baking powder

¼ teaspoon salt

½ teaspoon cinnamon

1 cup (2 sticks) plus 2 tablespoons salted butter, softened

1 cup plus 2 tablespoons light or dark brown sugar, firmly packed

½ cup plus 2 tablespoons granulated sugar

2 large eggs

½ teaspoon pure vanilla extract

1 cup old-fashioned rolled oats (not instant)

1¼ cups shredded coconut

DIRECTIONS

1. Preheat the oven to 325 degrees. Prepare cookie sheets with parchment.

2. In a small bowl combine the flour, baking soda, baking powder, salt, and cinnamon. Set aside.

3. In an electric mixer bowl, cream the butter, brown sugar, and granulated sugar until combined. Add the eggs and vanilla to the creamed mixture. Process until combined.

4. Add dry ingredients and process completely until a dough forms. Add oatmeal and shredded coconut. Process until combined.

5. Using an ice cream scoop or tablespoon (rounded), drop the dough one inch apart on prepared cookie sheets.

6. Bake 11-13 minutes, rotating the pans once during the baking cycle. The golden brown cookies will puff up nicely, but if you like chewier cookies (which I do), give the cookie sheet a quick tap on the stove top after you take it out of the oven. The cookies will instantly deflate and create a flatter, chewier cookie.

7. Transfer the cookies to a wire rack to cool completely.

Sharing

A Time for Sharing

k Don't you have a funny story involving Girl Scout cookies?

p Do you mean the one about my friend who said every major breakup has been during Girl Scout cookie season? She says to this day a box of Thin Mints can send her sobbing!

k Penny, that's hilarious. But you have a personal Girl Scout cookie story, don't you?

p Oh, yeah. It was on one of those cold days last spring and I decided I was going to spend it overeating and watching videos. I put on sweats and a ball cap to brave the elements to run and get the movies. It felt like my lucky day as I drove up to the video store and noticed the vendor table loaded with Girl Scout cookies for sale. After writing my check for half a dozen boxes of my favorite cookies, I glanced at the woman supervising the little Girl Scouts and casually asked her, "Don't I know you from somewhere?" With a giggle she replied, "Yes, I'm your Weight Watchers instructor."

I truly don't think it has ever occurred to me to keep my recipes a secret. When I'd been in business just a short time, Kitty Crider, the food editor of Austin's daily newspaper, called for a story. She wrote an impressive article and said later that one of the reasons was that I was willing to share my cookie recipes.

I must say others have a different viewpoint on this whole sharing issue. I will never forget how this came up in one of my cookie classes.

My good friend Evelyn has a friend, Wanda, who signed up to take one of my cookie classes. Days before the class, Wanda gave me a call at Penny's Pastries as a way of introduction. With a soft, whispering voice that carried the slightest Texas twang, Wanda told me of her life with cookies, especially tea cakes.

Since moving to Texas I have been intrigued with this whole tea cake thing. So many people have mentioned them to me with such fondness that I've always wanted a recipe for this regional favorite. So when Wanda mentioned her tea cakes I started to pay closer attention.

"Tea cakes, Wanda?" Is it a real homegrown formula? Is it a recipe you've been using for years?" I asked like the foodie I am.

"Oh, yes," was Wanda's reply. "I've had it all my life. Last year I made dozens of them to share with my family and friends. There's not a holiday that goes by without making my famous tea cakes."

"Gee, Wanda," I said, "I'd love to see the recipe." I waited for her response. And waited.

Finally Wanda replied, "I don't share the recipe with anyone. It's a secret that's been in my family for years."

With my recipe-sharing philosophy in mind, I replied, "I'd rethink that, Wanda. Recipes are for sharing, don't you think?"

She replied in a quiet voice, "I'll give it some thought."

Later that week, it was my pleasure to actually meet Wanda in our cookie class. She looked exactly as she sounded on the phone: pleasant and petite with a wonderful puff of pure white hair. As I went around the class acquainting myself with my students, I noticed

Wanda in the front row had her arm held high, fingers waving. Clearly she had something to say.

"Yes, Wanda," I acknowledged.

"You shamed me the other day," Wanda said with a smile.

She had captured my attention. "How did I shame you?" I asked.

In front of the class, Wanda relayed our telephone conversation. As she told the story, whenever she came to my part in our little chat, she dropped her Texas accent and imitated my voice expertly. It was the funniest thing. By the time she reached the point in our conversation where I suggested she rethink her sharing decision, the entire class, including me, was laughing.

What a cute, wonderful lady, I thought. Since that class, Wanda (who I usually run into at the post office) and I have become cookie friends. She now shares her wonderful tea cake recipe ("but not with just anybody"), and last year for the holidays, Wanda baked two thousand tea cakes in her home oven for family and friends. I'd call that a high level of sharing.

Sharing with Friends *as told by Matt Sessions*

When we were kids we used to visit my grandmother (whom we called Mom) in Hillsboro, Texas. One hot summer afternoon, my five-year-old cousin Leslie came inside the house and asked Mom if she could have a cookie for her buddies.

Mom asked, "Well how many buddies do you have, Leslie?"
Leslie replied, "Oh, 20 or 30."

And Mom said, "Goodness! I don't know if we have cookies for 20 or 30 of your friends!"

But Leslie quickly replied, "Mom, just one cookie would be fine."

By day, Matt, aka Metronome, manages the Cooking School at Breed & Company, but by night he is working in his dream job, as a drummer in several Austin bands. He inherited his love of cookies—and cooking—from his grandmother (they made cookies together when he was a child). Although he doesn't eat many cookies today, he does enjoy an occasional cookie from Penny's Pastries.

So Mom gave her one cookie and watched with curiosity as Leslie walked through the sliding glass door to the backyard and started to crumble the cookie. Mom went outside and said, "Leslie, what are you doing with your cookie?"

Leslie said, "I'm feeding it to my buddies." With her little fists tightly holding the cookie crumbs, she lifted both arms to the sky and released the sweet crumbs under the old oak trees. Then, with Mom by her side, she watched as all of her "bird buddies" quickly and eagerly nibbled at the cookie pieces.

Reaching Out *as told by Sandy Bobalik*

I was a young mother. One day my son brought over four or five friends to play. One kid seemed particularly shy and a little overwhelmed by the other rambunctious boys. He wandered into the kitchen where I was baking cookies. I asked him if he wanted to help me and he eagerly replied "Yes." So I got out additional cookie cutters and showed him how to roll the dough and cut the cookies. We sprinkled them with brightly colored sugars before baking. As the cookies came out of the oven his excitement over the freshly baked cookies was contagious!

Years later I ran into his mother at the shopping mall and she told me he still remembers our day of making and sharing cookies.

And the truth is, so do I.

If ever reincarnated, Sandy would like to come back as a pastry chef. In this life, Sandy spends her time helping her husband with his small business, caring for her granddaughter, and creating inspired cakes as a member of the Orlando (Florida) Cake Club. Lovingly called Cookie Monster by her husband, Sandy has been baking cookies all her life, first by light bulb in her Easy Bake Oven. With only one cookie rule (she only "dunks" lemon cookies), Sandy likes her cookies crisp and plentiful.

Cookie Ministry *as told by Willie Johnson*

My life changed profoundly in 1993. That was the year I went to the Ferguson Prison Unit in Huntsville, Texas. Feeling anxious and nervous, my stomach lurched as I heard the doors clank loudly behind me. I was there not as an inmate, but as a newly recruited volunteer for the Kairos Prison Ministry.

Although I had heard of this incredibly powerful interdenominational Christian program, which ministers to violent prisoners in state and federal correctional institutions, and the incredible results it generates (recidivism is reduced by up to 70% in participating prisons), I was in no way prepared for the life-changing experience it would become for me. My own father was murdered in 1987, and volunteering at the prison would mean that I would work with, sit next to, talk

Willie (known to some people as "Smokie") Johnson loves peanut butter cookies almost as much as he loves being a granddad to Jamille. In fact, his favorite saying these days is, "If I knew that being a granddaddy was this good, I would have skipped being a dad!" A native Texan, Willie is a project manager in information technology today, but is in the process of defining his dream job—retirement.

to, and forgive other hardened criminals like the one whose indescribable act of malice forever altered my place on this planet.

Kairos, affectionately called the "Cookie Ministry," uses cookies as a symbol of love given to a people who seldom encounter such a gift in their daily lives. Some haven't had a homemade cookie in upwards of 15 years, and for almost all of them this is the only "homemade" food they will receive in prison.

Each Kairos team is responsible for providing 5,000 dozen homemade cookies, which are doled out daily to each member of the prison population, including inmates and employees (even inmates in solitary confinement). These cookies cannot be purchased anywhere at any price because the cookies bring a Christian message: "I am worth someone baking homemade cookies for me. People love and care for me, despite what I've done."

It's amazing what happens when you show unconditional love in the form of a homemade cookie. The inmates are touched and they are changed. The truth is, we all are.

The Cookie Thief *by Valerie Cox*

A woman was waiting at an airport one night
With several long hours before her flight
She hunted for a book in the airport shop
Bought a bag of cookies and found a place to drop

She was engrossed in her book but happened to see
That the man beside her—as bold as could be—
Grabbed a cookie or two from the bag between
Which she tried to ignore to avoid a scene

She munched cookies and watched the clock
As the gutsy cookie thief diminished her stock
She was getting more irritated as the minutes ticked by
Thinking "If I wasn't so nice, I'd blacken his eye."

With each cookie she took, he took one, too
When only one was left, she wondered what he'd do
With a smile on his face and a nervous laugh
He took the last cookie and broke it in half

Valerie Cox, author, poet, world-traveler and lifetime fan of cookies, lives on the West Coast. Her poem "The Cookie Thief" was written in 1988 and first appeared in print in A 3rd Serving of Chicken Soup for the Soul.

He offered her half as he ate the other
She snatched it from him and thought "Oh, Brother!
This guy has some nerve, and he's also rude
Why, he didn't even show any gratitude!"

She had never known when she had been so galled
And sighed with relief when her flight was called
She gathered her belongings and headed to the gate
Refusing to look back at that thieving ingrate

She boarded the plane and sank in her seat
Then sought her book, which was almost complete
As she reached in her baggage, she gasped with surprise
There was her bag of cookies in front of her eyes

If mine are here, she moaned with despair
Then the others were his, and he tried to share!
Too late to apologize, she realized with grief
That she was the rude one, the ingrate, the thief!

Penny Suggests: Cookies for Sharing

One of my most important life principles is to show value and appreciation of all people regardless of life station or ethnicity. Practiced by both my parents, reinforced through friends like Kathy, and many of my cookie customers, a heart-felt appreciation of people keeps us connected and centered. And what better way to show that appreciation than by sharing a batch of warm, homemade cookies.

All-American Brownies

When I moved to Austin from Washington, D.C., I felt like an outsider, so I signed up for a cake-decorating class, hoping to make connections. The instructor was a woman who not only shared this wonderful brownie recipe, but more importantly, became my friend and my first employee. With its thick layer of chocolate frosting and toasted pecans, this brownie is one of Sharon's delicious contributions to my life. Any time I bake them, I think of the early days, working with Sharon deep into the night, laughing, and creating an enduring friendship.

Yield: One 13" x 9" pan
Temperature: 325 degrees
Baking Time: 35-40 minutes

INGREDIENTS

6 large eggs
3 cups granulated sugar
1½ cups (3 sticks) salted butter (or margarine)
2 teaspoons pure vanilla extract
2 cups all-purpose flour
⅓ cup cocoa

ICING

¼ cup whole milk or cream
½ cup (1 stick) salted butter
3¾ cups powdered sugar
⅛ cup cocoa
1 tablespoon pure vanilla extract
Toasted walnut or pecan pieces

DIRECTIONS

1. Preheat oven to 325 degrees. Line 13" x 9" pan with foil and spray with non-stick cooking spray. Set aside.

2. Put eggs in electric mixer bowl. Add sugar and vanilla. Process until mixed.

3. Melt the butter and add it to the egg and sugar mixture. Process.

4. Add flour and cocoa. Process until thin batter is formed.

5. Pour batter into prepared baking pan and bake 35-40 minutes, rotating the pan once during the baking cycle. The brownie is fully baked when the sides are firm and the middle is set.

ICING

1. While the brownie is baking, melt butter with milk. Pour into mixer bowl and let cool.

2. Add powdered sugar and cocoa to cooled mixture. Process until smooth. Add vanilla.

3. While brownie is cooling, but still warm, spread frosting.

4. Before icing has a chance to set, sprinkle with toasted pecans or walnuts. Let cool before cutting into squares.

Oatmeal Fudge Bars

A first-rate brownie to take and share at any gathering from book group to game night. There are several steps you must go through to get to the finished bars, but oh, what a sweet journey. Chewy, chocolatey, with that oatmeal cookie base, they keep well and travel well.

Yield: One 13" x 9" pan
Temperature: 325 degrees
Baking Time: 35-40 minutes

INGREDIENTS

BOTTOM/TOP LAYER
9 tablespoons (1 stick plus 1T) salted butter

$1\frac{1}{2}$ cups light or dark brown sugar, firmly packed

2 large eggs

1 tablespoon pure vanilla extract

$1\frac{1}{2}$ cups all-purpose flour

$1\frac{3}{4}$ teaspoons baking powder

$2\frac{1}{4}$ cups old-fashioned oats (not instant)

CHOCOLATE LAYER
$1\frac{1}{2}$ tablespoons salted butter

9 ounces ($1\frac{1}{2}$ cups) semisweet chocolate chips

$\frac{3}{4}$ cup sweetened condensed milk

1 tablespoon pure vanilla extract

DIRECTIONS

1. Preheat oven to 325 degrees. Line 13" x 9" pan with foil and spray with non-stick cooking spray. Set aside.

2. In an electric mixer bowl, cream the butter with the brown sugar. Add the eggs and vanilla. Process until combined.

3. In a separate bowl, mix the flour with the baking powder and oats.

4. Add the dry ingredients to the creamed ingredients. Using your hands or the back of a spoon, press two-thirds of this mixture into the bottom of the prepared pan.

5. In a small pan, melt the butter, chocolate, and condensed milk. When the mixture is smooth and thick, remove from the heat and stir in vanilla.

6. Spread this fudge-like chocolate mixture evenly over the pressed oatmeal layer.

7. By rounded teaspoons, drop the remaining third of the oatmeal mixture evenly over the chocolate mixture.

8. Bake in the upper third of the preheated oven for approximately 35-40 minutes, rotating the pan once during the baking cycle.

9. Remove pan from oven and let cool completely before cutting into bars.

Wanda's Tea Cakes

When I called to ask Wanda if she was ready to share her recipe with the world through Cookie Stories she said "Yes" without hesitation. So here without further explanation is Wanda's tea cake recipe exactly the way she gave it to me. If made with as much loving care as Wanda gives these cookies, they're sure to be a big hit.

Yield: 2 dozen cookies
Temperature: 375 degrees
Baking Time: 11-14 minutes

INGREDIENTS

2½ cups all-purpose flour

1 teaspoon baking soda

½ teaspoon salt

½ cup vegetable shortening

1¼ cup granulated sugar

1 large egg

2 tablespoons pure vanilla extract

1 cup sour cream

(Note: Wanda says she used to use 1 teaspoon vanilla "like it was law" until she took my cookie class. Since then she's increased the vanilla to 2 tablespoons and "boy, does that make a difference.")

DIRECTIONS

1. Preheat oven to 375 degrees. Prepare baking pan. (Wanda prepares the pan by wiping it lightly with shortening. I'd probably use parchment, but who am I to argue with Wanda?)

2. In a small bowl, sift the flour with baking soda and salt. Set aside.

3. Cream shortening and sugar in mixer until smooth. Add egg and vanilla. Process until smooth. Add sour cream and process.

4. Add dry ingredients to form a soft cookie dough.

5. Refrigerate until "good and cold." Using a small ice cream scoop, form cookies one inch apart on cookie sheet.

6. Bake 11-14 minutes or until bottoms of cookies are golden brown and tops are blond.

Wanda says for an added touch and a little additional sweetness you can sprinkle the cookies with crystal sugar before baking. Or after the cookies have cooled they can be covered with a little cookie glaze. Wanda likes to tint the glaze pink.

Reba's Oatmeal Raisin Cookies

I met Reba at a local catering company where she was the kitchen coordinator. We immediately hit it off and have, over the years, created a connection that I absolutely treasure. Years ago I asked her for her oatmeal raisin cookie recipe. She generously shared this wonderful, spicy formula with me. Also great with chopped dates instead of raisins.

Yield: 3-4 dozen cookies
Temperature: 325 degrees
Baking Time: 12-13 minutes

INGREDIENTS

½ cup (1 stick) salted butter, softened

½ cup vegetable shortening

1 cup light or dark brown sugar, firmly packed

1 cup granulated sugar

1 tablespoon honey

2 large eggs

1 teaspoon pure vanilla extract

1½ cups all-purpose flour

1 teaspoon ground cinnamon

1 teaspoon salt

1 teaspoon baking soda

2 cups old-fashioned oats (not instant)

1 cup walnuts or pecans, chopped

1 cup dried fruit (golden or dark raisins, apricots, dates, etc.)

DIRECTIONS

1. Preheat oven to 325 degrees. Prepare cookie sheets with kitchen parchment.

2. In electric mixer bowl, combine butter, shortening, and both sugars. Cream on low speed until smooth.

3. Add liquid ingredients (including honey) to creamed mixture. Mix until incorporated.

4. In a separate bowl, mix flour, cinnamon, salt, and baking soda.

5. Add the dry ingredients to the mixer bowl and combine until dough forms.

6. Add oatmeal to mixer bowl. Mix until incorporated. Add nuts and dried fruit and combine.

7. Portion dough by rounded tablespoons or use ice cream scoop. Place cookies one inch apart on prepared cookie sheets. Lightly press the cookie balls down with your fingertips before baking.

8. Bake 12-13 minutes, rotating pans once during the baking cycle. Finished cookies will come from the oven puffy and golden brown.

9. Transfer cookies to a wire rack to cool.

Holidays

Holiday Memories

k Ever since I was a kid I've loved holidays.

p Me, too. They've always been magical to me. And so much fun!

k It's that one time of year when everyone comes home and we have yummy food, special cookies, and those festive twinkling lights.

p And we all get to tell the same family stories year after year.

k Don't you think it's funny that every family has a secret language built on its own quirky traditions and holiday memories? When someone in the family asks, "Remember that Christmas blessing Mom gave five years ago?" everyone knows exactly what that means and we all burst out laughing.

p Oh, yeah, I love that part. We never get tired of them. We laugh like it's the first time we've ever heard the story.

I remember when Al and I were planning our first trip back home to Michigan for the holidays. We'd been married less than a year and had moved shortly after our Michigan wedding to Colorado Springs, Colorado. Though I'd had countless long-distance conversations with my parents, sisters, and friends, I hadn't seen them since the wedding. In less than a week, we'd be going home for the holidays; I simply couldn't wait.

"Why are you still awake?" Al asked, adjusting his pillows. It was the middle of the night a few days before we were to leave, and I couldn't get to sleep.

"I'm just excited about going home for Christmas," I replied, hedging. But that wasn't the only reason I couldn't sleep. As delighted as I was at the prospect of seeing my family again, I also realized we'd be going home empty-handed. Being newlyweds, we had very little money, and though we'd scraped together the airfare, there simply wasn't anything left for buying Christmas presents.

"Well, try and get some sleep," Al said as he patted my shoulder, rolled onto his favorite sleeping side, and promptly fell back to sleep.

It wasn't as if I hadn't been trying before, but obviously I needed to try harder. I lay down on my back, pulled the blankets under my chin, and listened to our small space heater hum. I felt my eyelids getting heavy as I released the tension in my body and finally relaxed. I was almost asleep when one word blazed in my brain: cookies. I could make tons of cookies and take them home as gifts.

If I couldn't sleep when I had the problem, now the solution was pure adrenaline. I sat straight up, knowing I had cookies to design and bake. "Where are my cutters?" I mumbled to myself. "Do we have butter, enough flour?" I wondered. I had work to do and only two days to do it, I thought. I must get to work. Now.

Jumping out of bed, I ran to our small kitchen, climbed the step stool, and pulled down my shoebox of cookie cutters from the cupboard over the refrigerator. Like a woman possessed, I tore through the box searching for just the right cutter.

"Angels!" I almost screamed into the night, so far past excited I must have looked crazed. I held the angel cookie cutter like it was a gift from the gods. I'd make angels for everyone, and after baking and decorating the cookies, I'd pack them in the small baskets and tins we had around the house.

Butter, I thought, flinging open the refrigerator; I need lots of butter. There, on the bottom shelf, I spotted several pounds. We had eggs, too—I almost cried.

I gathered all the ingredients on the kitchen counter and entered a world of my own, making batch after batch of butter cookie dough. My mission had taken on a life of its own. I needed music.

I simply love to bake, sing, and dance to popular music, mostly rhythm and blues, specifically Aretha Franklin. My mother used to call me her Singing Baker. She said you could always tell when I was in the kitchen, even as a little girl, because you could hear me singing. So, with rubber spatula in hand and thick socks covering my feet, dressed in my nightshirt and a flour-covered apron, I slid into our tiny living room to crank it up.

"Take me to heart and I'll always love you," Aretha crooned. I swiveled my hips to the soulful sound, closed my eyes, and threw back my head to sing along. I was so in my element I didn't notice Al leaning against our open bedroom door, wearing only his boxer shorts, staring at me in disbelief.

"What are you doing?" he asked, sounding almost frightened. "Penny, do you realize what time it is?" he continued as he walked across the room to turn the stereo down. His eye caught the light in the kitchen, and without asking another question, he moved toward it. His jaw dropped and his eyes grew big as plates at the sight within: mixing bowls filled with cookie dough and counter tops piled with cookie sheets, little vials of color, and empty egg cartons. The oven was hot, and cupboards stood open. He turned around and looked at me, concern written on his face.

I rushed to explain. "Al, I had a great idea," I said with a smile as I squeezed past him into my sanctuary. "I thought we could take cookies home to the family. Angel cookies, Al. Pretty angel cookies. I'll bake them and pack them in tins with pastel tissue paper. They'll look great. I am so excited!"

"Yes, Penny, there's no question about your excitement; it's so very obvious. But it's four in the morning," he said gently. "Four in the morning," he repeated, this time locking my eyes with his.

"But we leave in two days," I responded in my own defense. "There's so much to do, and I have so little time."

"Okay, I get it," he said, unconvincingly. "Just try and keep it down."

"Sure, I can do that. Why don't you go back to bed and get some sleep. I'll be in soon," I lied.

With that he gave me what was supposed to be an understanding smile and went to bed, closing the door behind him and leaving me to my own world.

Once Al was back in the bedroom, I tiptoed back to the living room to reconnect with Aretha. I turned the volume up just a tiny bit and went back to doing what I do best, baking and decorating.

The cookies turned out beautifully: simple angels held red frosting hearts, fanciful angels wore crystal sugar and silver-covered candies, and humble angels folded their pristine white wings. Packed carefully, the delicate cookies made it home with their glory intact.

Spending the holidays at home with our families filled me with delight. Those few days went by too fast, but I can still see the look in my mother's eyes as she pulled back the tissue on her angels and gave her Singing Baker a kiss and a hug of appreciation.

A Chocolate Chip Ritual *as told by Lee Carnes*

I can't remember a childhood Christmas that did not revolve around my grandmother, my cousin Jenny, and me baking chocolate chip cookies for Santa. It was as important a ritual as opening presents on Christmas morning. The three of us made a great baking team, and even though my grandmother had strict rules about the amount of chocolate chips we could use, she always made sure there was enough cookie dough left to make licking the bowl worthwhile.

If it's a cold winter's night, or a late spring rain storm, you'll find Lee in bed wearing her PJs, covered by her favorite blanket, engrossed in a movie or reading a good book. By her side will be a plate of warm chocolate chip cookies and ice-cold milk. Lee, an event planner, dreams of one day becoming a travel writer and calls both Denver, Colorado, and El Paso, Texas, home. An only child, from as far back as she can remember both Lee and her mother call each other DeeDee, while the good folks of her second hometown El Paso still refer to her as "Chili con Carne."

Recently I bought a beautiful shiny red mixer. I wanted to break it in by making something special. I searched through my cookbooks until it hit me. I went to the store, and bought the necessary ingredients to make those time-honored chocolate chip cookies. Unlike my childhood Christmas baking sessions with Grammy, I allowed myself to double the amount of chocolate chips in the recipe. Adulthood has its rewards!

Cookie Espionage *as told by Fran Koehler*

If my memory serves me correctly, we either made the cookie dough in the sink or in a pickle bucket. I just remember pounds and pounds of dough … and then the espionage! It was always a challenge to be able to sneak "a hot one" right out of the oven before Dad began the "counting of the cookies." He knew down to the last "ant load" how many of those delectable chocolate cookies resided in that Christmas tin. Woe betide the brazen burglar!

For Dad there was nothing worse than returning home from an exhausting Christmas shopping spree, unloading and hiding all of the gifts, all in the hopes of sitting down to a cold glass of milk and, yes, my friend, a light, almost hollow-sounding Christmas tin of despair! Oh the agony of it all. Crumbs here and there, chips overturned … and good God, a cookie with teeth marks!! Those nine urchins of Tyson Drive had struck! What was a father to do? Grab the pound cake and run!!!!

Fran, originally from St. Louis, grew up with eight other cookie-loving siblings. Making cookies in her family was truly an event— imagine the amount of dough that was required to make cookies in a house of 11 people. No wonder her rule for cookie-eating is "Must eat every last crumb!" Now a wife and mother of five, Fran has given birth to a new generation of cookie enthusiasts.

Reindeer Legs *as told by Lori Galindo*

Ever since I was a small child, I've always loved to cook and bake. Every year at Christmas time, we would get together at Grandma's and bake Christmas cookies. My grandmother's sister, Tia Rita (who was probably in her 60s at the time), joined us one year. This was an especially fun time because several of my cousins were there along with my sisters and me. We sang Christmas carols and told funny stories and were just having a great time gathered around Grandma's kitchen table rolling cookies. Tia Rita even joined in and decided to transfer the cookies we had cut out onto the baking sheets. No one really paid attention to her technique, but we did notice she was taking some dough off of some of them. After the cookies came out of the oven, we realized that the reindeer-shaped cookies were all missing their legs! Tia Rita had cut them off. To this day, we don't know what made her decide to cut off those reindeer legs, but for some funny reason they just didn't look right to her. It's a family mystery we've never solved, but it still gives us great laughs.

Originally from Pharr, Texas (in the Rio Grande Valley), Lori has lived in Austin 15 years. Her favorite cookie memory is walking home from elementary school with her buddy Manuel, because he would share his leftover lunch-time cookies with her, and his mom made THE best cookies. A baker since the age of three, she likes crunchy but soft cookies, and her favorite is chocolate chip cookies.

Burnt Camels *as told by Robert Ballew*

My family used to get together at Christmas time to make basic shortbread cookies and decorate them. This went on from childhood through college age—three kids and my Mom, every year. We'd make up cookie baskets and fill them with the shapes of the season—bells, stars, camels—to give to friends and relatives in Lubbock, Texas, where we lived. As the rest of us would concentrate on the rolling and cutting and baking, my brother's job (he was the most artistic of the family) was to take the frosting squeezer and make various decorative floral designs, such as hollies and berries.

We didn't pay too much attention to what he was doing because he usually did a great job. However, one year a batch of cut-out camels stayed in the oven too long, and unbeknownst to us all, he wrote "burnt" across the camels in

Robert, otherwise known as Babaloo, a self-described Texitalian, says his dream job would involve traveling with his family to Europe (especially Italy) to collect recipes (including cookie recipes) for a cookbook. A proponent of simply elegant, rich-tasting cookies, Robert's favorite is a French or Italian tea cake, which he prefers to eat in the morning with a café latte. The family's favorite cookie recipe is a French butter cookie recipe given to them by Antoinette, a dear family friend.

red frosting. This batch of rejects somehow got added to someone's Christmas basket instead. Around New Year's we received a package. It was one of the burnt camels mounted in a frame, returned to us as a gift. We thought it was hilarious.

It's now a 25-year-old cookie and still hangs in my brother's house. Its leg has fallen off and the frosting has hardened, but the burnt camel is legend among my family and friends and still merits a chuckle even today.

Bourbon Balls *as told by Diana Alsup Gielstra*

My mother, Diane, was not the world's greatest cook. On the contrary, her kitchen was in perfect order because she seldom cooked—with the exception of microwave burritos, canned soup, and oven-warmed chicken pot pies you could buy three for $1 from the grocery store freezer section. (To my chagrin, she always stocked up on the latter!)

But during the Christmas season everything changed. She went from a liberated feminist to a modern day Martha Stewart, baking, roasting, and stewing any and everything that her cupboard held. And out of this cooking mayhem, my brother and I eagerly anticipated her baking our most favorite cookie of all, her famous bourbon balls.

Diana considers herself a very traditional cookie eater. "I enjoy eating cookies right out of the oven with a glass of cold milk." The more butter, the more chocolate, the better. Originally from Conway, South Carolina, she is currently a PhD student and a research scientist in Austin, Texas. (We're secretly hoping she'll decide to research new types of cookies!)

Our pulses would quicken as she poured the vanilla wafers into a long pan, covered it with wax paper, and pounded away with a mallet to achieve a fine crumbled mass. Then she sprinkled a strong bitter Dutch cocoa over it all as if it were pixie dust. Then came the corn syrup. Finally, as we watched wide-eyed, clinging to the kitchen counter and holding our breath, she measured the quarter cup of bourbon, and poured it on top. She'd always look at us, wink, and add an extra splash just for kicks.

We would dance around the kitchen humming Christmas tunes as she shaped them with her hands, each one a perfect sphere that she threw into a bin of powdered sugar. They were perfect little snowballs. She placed them into tin after tin for gifts, and for us she placed a few into a crystal Christmas tree-shaped container. She placed the crystal tree on the corner of a den side table and would monitor us as we ate the one cookie we were allowed to have. As children, we always thought she was a genius, as it was quite chic to eat something so sinful on such a saintly holiday. As the grown-ups would toast with their wine and my grandfather told us stories about his childhood Christmases, my brother and I would each sneak an extra bourbon ball and try to clink them together the same way the grown-ups did for their toast. Instead of clinking, the cookies would leave a white powder on the carpet that was sure to get us in trouble later.

As an adult I now realize my mother's genius in these cookies was how simple they were to make. There is no cooking involved, and that was just her style. My mother passed away many years ago, but even today I receive calls from my father, grandfather, and brother to make each of them bourbon balls at Christmas. As I shape each ball, I hum Christmas tunes, and, well, sometimes, I still dance around the kitchen.

Ya Ya Honey's Greek Cookies *as told by John Males*

My great-grandmother, Ya Ya Honey, was considered by many people to be an unbelievable cook, and she considered herself to be the finest cook there ever was. She would boast that she did the "best of" this and the "best of" that. She was very proud of her desserts, especially her Kourambiethes, the traditional round Greek cookie with powdered sugar and one clove on top. Although difficult to make and very labor intensive, she would make them to perfection, so uniform they looked like they were made in a professional bakery. Then she'd gently place them in a box layered with tissue.

One Christmas many years ago, my granny was having people over for the holidays, so she asked Ya Ya Honey to make these special cookies for the occasion. My grandmother

People who meet John like him immediately, which is why he's so successful as a consultant, speaker, and entrepreneur. Most people don't know this about him, but John has a personal tradition of buying a half-dozen freshly baked (chunky) oatmeal raisin cookies (his favorite) at Weikel's Bakery (a family-owned bakery located between Austin and Houston) and consuming them all on his way to visit various clients in Houston. He says (and we believe him) the cookies fuel his creativity. Originally from Detroit, his personal motto is: You can't steer unless you're driving!

told my grandfather, "Go in the car to Mom's house, and she's going to give you a box of her specialty cookies. Bring them back for the party tonight."

My grandfather was an extremely clumsy man. In fact, he was so clumsy it was the stuff of family legends. He could trip, literally, over something that wasn't there. On this day he went to Ya Ya Honey's house to fetch the cookies. She carefully handed him the box saying, "Here they are, Leonard. Please be careful." As he turned to leave, his shoe caught on one of the cracks in the sidewalk, causing the box to fly out of his hands and land with such force that the cookies shattered into pieces. Ya Ya Honey, standing in the doorway, yelled Greek curses at him as he attempted to jam the cookies back into the box. "No worry, Ma," he yelled back at her. "I'll eat the broken ones!"

Penny Suggests: Holiday Cookies

Holiday baking is the best. If you don't bake at any other time of the year this is the time to put the diet gelatin away and bring out the mixing bowl. You know it's holiday time when the smell of vanilla and peppermint is in the air, you're busy making lists and sorting through cookie cutters, and family and friends start gathering for celebration.

 # Peppermint Penny

We make this brownie only during the holidays at Penny's. I love the light chocolate/peppermint combination. Not as rich as most brownies, it's company-ready with just a slight drizzle of melted chocolate and crushed peppermint candy.

Yield: One 13" x 9" pan
Temperature: 325 degrees
Baking Time: 50-55 minutes

INGREDIENTS

1 cup crushed peppermint candy

2 cups all-purpose flour

1 teaspoon baking powder

6 large eggs

1 teaspoon pure vanilla extract

1 teaspoon peppermint extract

1 cup (2 sticks) plus 2 tablespoons salted butter

3 1/3 cups semisweet chocolate chips, separated

2 cups granulated sugar

FINISH

1/2 cup semisweet chocolate chips, melted

1/4 cup crushed peppermint candy

DIRECTIONS

1. Preheat oven to 325 degrees. Line pan with foil and spray with non-stick cooking spray. Set aside.

2. Put unwrapped peppermint candy in a plastic bag. Cover bag with a kitchen towel. Crush candy using a hammer or a rolling pin until the candy is in tiny pieces. Set candy aside, reserving $1/4$ cup for finish.

3. Mix flour and baking powder. Set aside.

4. In another small bowl, combine eggs, vanilla, and peppermint extract. Set aside.

5. Melt butter in microwave or double boiler. While still hot, add $1 1/3$ cups chocolate chips to butter and stir until chips are completely melted.

6. Put sugar into an electric mixer bowl. Add melted chocolate mixture to sugar and process until mixed. Add eggs and extracts to mixer bowl and process.

7. Add dry ingredients to mixer bowl. Mix until smooth and brownie batter is formed.

8. Fold remaining 2 cups of chocolate chips and 1 cup crushed candy into the batter.

9. Pour batter into baking pan and bake 50-55 minutes, rotating once during baking cycle. Brownie is fully baked when the sides are completely set and toothpick inserted one inch from sides comes out slightly coated.

FINISH

After brownie has cooled, drizzle with $1/2$ cup melted chocolate chips. (An easy way to do this is to put the melted chocolate in a plastic bag. Cut a tip off one corner of the bag and force the chocolate through the hole.) Before chocolate has a chance to set, sprinkle with reserved crushed candy.

 # Fruit and Nut Cups

When I started my first bakery in Washington, D.C., it was with an original cake recipe I made for my father. Over time I adjusted that cake formula to create this cookie. Baked in the disposable aluminum tart tins available at your local grocery, these chewy confections are loaded with plump raisins and apricots. Give these as gifts in a tissue-lined basket or serve at home while trimming the tree.

Yield: 16 tarts
Temperature: 350 degrees
Baking Time: 13-15 minutes

INGREDIENTS

4 large eggs

2⅓ cups light or dark brown sugar, firmly packed

1 teaspoon salt

1 teaspoon pure vanilla extract

1 teaspoon lemon extract

2 cups all-purpose flour

⅓ cup dark raisins

⅓ cup golden raisins

⅓ cup dried apricots, chopped

2 cups pecans, chopped

DIRECTIONS

1. Preheat oven to 350 degrees. Place tart tins on baking sheets. Spray them generously with an even coat of non-stick cooking spray. Set aside.

2. In a large mixing bowl using a rubber spatula or an electric mixer, combine eggs, brown sugar, salt, and flavorings. Mix until smooth.

3. Add flour to sugar and egg mixture. Combine until cookie batter forms.

4. Fold in dried fruit and nuts by hand until completely integrated.

5. Using a large spoon, divide mixture evenly between prepared tart tins.

6. Bake 13-15 minutes, rotating once during the baking cycle. Cookie cups are ready when middle is set, but not dry, and tops are shiny. Let cookie cups cool completely before releasing from cookie tins.

Penny's Roll and Cut Recipe

I have been a cookie cutter collector for over twenty years. With a collection that now numbers in the thousands (5,000!), we have great fun cutting and decorating cookies. This is the recipe we developed at Penny's Pastries for our signature line of decorated cookies. You're going to love using this dough in your home kitchen because it's easy to put together, doesn't require refrigeration before using, cuts like a dream, is perfect for making decorated masterpieces, and the finished cookies are simply delicious.

Yield: 3-4 dozen cookies
Temperature: 325 degrees
Baking Time: 8-10 minutes

INGREDIENTS

2 cups salted butter

2 cups granulated sugar

2 large eggs

4 tablespoons whipping cream or whole milk

4 tablespoons pure vanilla extract

2 teaspoons almond extract

6 cups all-purpose flour

1 tablespoon baking powder

ROYAL FROSTING

6 tablespoons warm water

3 tablespoons meringue powder*

3 1/2 cups powdered sugar, sifted

1/4 teaspoon cream of tartar (optional)

1/2 teaspoon flavoring such as almond extract, orange extract, or lemon extract (optional)

*Buy meringue powder at cake decorating stores.

DIRECTIONS

1. Preheat oven to 325 degrees. Prepare cookie sheets with kitchen parchment.

2. In electric mixer bowl, mix butter with sugar until smooth. Remember to just incorporate these ingredients, do not cream until light.

3. Add all liquid ingredients to bowl and process.

4. In a separate bowl, mix flour with baking powder.

5. Add the dry ingredients all at once to the mixer bowl and process until heavy dough forms.

6. To prepare the dough for rolling and cutting, separate the finished dough into two large balls. Work with one dough ball at a time.

7. Flour a work surface. Knead the dough a few times to smooth it out before rolling.

8. Re-flour the surface if necessary. Sprinkle a light dusting of flour directly on the dough surface. With a rolling pin, roll dough in a disk until the dough is approximately ¼" thick.

(Roll dough thicker if you prefer a more cake-like texture to the finished cookies.)

Remember while you're rolling to occasionally lift the dough from the work surface and turn it so it will not stick. Add additional flour to the work surface when necessary.

9. Cut into desired shapes with cookie cutters. The dough scraps can be used several times.

10. Bake 8-10 minutes, rotating pans once during the baking cycle. The cookies are perfect when the bottoms are golden brown and the tops are light blond.

11. Cool completely on a wire rack before decorating.

ROYAL FROSTING

1. Pour warm water into electric mixer bowl. Add all other ingredients.

2. With speed on low, mix ingredients until they form a thick frosting.

3. When the icing is smooth, set the mixer on its highest setting and process until the icing goes from shiny to dull, has doubled in volume, and will stand in stiff peaks.

4. Separate the finished frosting into small (preferably glass, or disposable) bowls. Tint the frosting with professional-quality gel colors as desired.

5. Spread the frosting onto the cookies using small, off-set cake spatulas. The finished cookies can also be dipped into the frosting if you want cookies with a smoother finish. If you prefer this method, mix a little water into the finished frosting to create a thinner consistency (think cinnamon roll glaze). When the cookie base frosting is set, the cookies can be further decorated with additional Royal frosting forced through a pastry bag with fitted pastry tip.

Note: After you make the icing, keep it covered with a damp cloth at all times (even after you have tinted it and put it in a pastry bag) or it will crust over. This icing is not a "keeper." It does not have a long shelf-life at this stage so make just as much as you need.

Cookie Wisdom

Cookies Yield Life Lessons

When Penny's Pastries decided to publish all the cookie, brownie, and shortbread recipes in *Cookie Stories,* we faced a daunting task. All those commercial-sized formulas needed to be scaled down for use in a home kitchen. We hired a professional recipe tester for the conversions, but they also needed to be tested by home bakers so we'd be sure the recipes were easy to follow and fun to use.

One wintry day several months before Christmas, Kathy and I came up with an inspired idea. We'd use some of our friends to test the recipes by hosting an old-fashioned cookie exchange. We'd give them the recipes along with instructions and a cookie survey. They'd bake the cookies in their home kitchens, then meet us for the cookie exchange, where we'd hear their feedback, sip hot cocoa, munch on cookies, and talk girl talk.

After the invitations went out and the calls started coming in, we realized this would be no ordinary event, but a memory maker. Not only were there problems with the recipes (still much too large for a home kitchen), but the personal doubts from our friends-turned-recipe testers were nothing short of comical. Most of these women are in professional careers, and their days are filled with strategy sessions and networking as opposed to manipulating oven temperatures or debating the merits of salted versus unsalted butter. Needless to say, they were feeling some heavy-duty baking anxiety.

Despite all of the baking and recipe problems, phone counseling, and contingency planning, the cookie party turned out to be a lively affair with lots of sharing. Most of our home bakers were actually able to bring their finished cookies and brownies, but I must say the person who takes the prize for perseverance has got to be Diana, who tested the brownies we call Peppermint Pennys. Filled with some of the same doubts and frustrations as the other women, she pushed through and gave us an award-winning effort. Her recipe, calling for cups of crushed peppermint candy and mounds of cocoa powder, produced a brownie big enough for half the state of Texas with leftovers. On the day of the event she flew in the door, cheeks pink from baking this monster brownie, still in its baking pan cooling on a wooden bookshelf. I can just imagine her before the exchange, frantic with her hot brownie, throwing books on the floor and ripping that board from the case. We said we needed a Peppermint Penny

tested, and by gosh, she was going to test a Peppermint Penny. As it turns out her brownie tasted wonderful; she baked it to perfection. But even more importantly, her attitude was incredibly refreshing. She, along with our other friends working through their baking issues, gave Kathy and me a very lively cookie exchange and a wonderful new cookie story.

Believe me, the perseverance that Diana displayed with the brownie is the same type that's gotten me through my own cookie mistakes. If I'd ever stopped baking cookies because of botched batches, I'd have closed Penny's Pastries years ago.

To illustrate my point, I remember one day coming home completely defeated. It had been a challenging day at the bakery as my staff and I worked on new cookie formulas for the upcoming year-end sales. With all the ovens fired up, the kitchen was memorably hot, yet we worked tirelessly and with great passion on our new cookie offerings. From somewhere in the middle of my creativity, I had the notion of inventing a heavenly bittersweet chocolate brownie infused with a spicy white chocolate swirl, finished with toasted hazelnuts. What we got instead, for all of our marathon baking, was brownie failure. At the end of the day, with test batches of half-eaten brownies covering the kitchen, I stood there, looked into their faces of defeat and knew with certainty we'd have to call it a day. So with a dramatic flourish I took off my apron, cut off small squares of test brownies to take with me, and patted their slumped shoulders as a show of support as I made my exit.

When I got home I took a quick shower, pulled on clean shorts and a T-shirt and curled up in my favorite chair to relax. But those brownie samples on my kitchen counter kept calling me. Finally I scooped up the four little plastic-wrapped failures and took a seat on our patio. One after the other I opened the brownies and tasted a small piece. Still not good. I laid my head back and closed my eyes to the fading sun to think. I could not figure out what was wrong. But in my brownie despair, I had a thought. My eyes popped open and I sat upright. I'd had an epiphany.

What I realized from some crazed place in my tired brain was that the brownies were not a failure at all, but instead a wonderful, fabulous, valuable life lesson. What I got was that my entire baking journey—from my childhood days with my mother and sisters, to college, marriage, twins, divorce, sadness, passion, love, and laughter—has been ripe with life lessons.

So now, with this newfound energy, I threw the samples in the trash and picked up my pad to record my lessons learned from a cookie.

Life Lesson #1: Cookies crumble.

Tires flatten. Hair has bad days. Plans go unrealized. Nothing unique here—learn to elegantly move on.

Life Lesson #2: The value is in the sharing, not the stirring.

There are bags of prepared cookies already on the store shelf or cookie dough in the refrigerator section of every grocery store. Does anybody really care if you sift the flour, chop the nuts by hand, and cream the butter? Probably not. Whatever you have, share generously.

Life Lesson #3: Live life creatively.

Go ahead and live with one foot outside the box. Frost elephants purple or Christmas trees pink. Don't bind your life with how things should be or follow the status quo. Go a little crazy and live life creatively.

Life Lesson #4: Some of the best cookies start with humble beginnings.

Simple flour, sugar, and butter make great-tasting cookies. Life is not about expensive trinkets; it's about how you leverage what you have.

Life Lesson #5: You're never too old to discover white chocolate.

So you grew up consuming chocolate chip, oatmeal raisin, and peanut butter cookies. Come out of your comfort zone. Live a little, have a new experience.

Life Lesson #6: Don't judge a cookie by its shape, color, or size.

Okay, so it looks different to you. You think it's too fat, flat, plain, or flawed. Be daring, try it anyway. You may be pleasantly surprised. Don't live life by making assumptions from the sidelines—jump in and participate.

Life Lesson #7: Savor every succulent bite.

With every sensual bite, thoroughly enjoy life. Love deeply and passionately.

Life Lesson #8: Everyone gets to dream.

Cookies made from seaweed and cinnamon? So maybe it's not for you. But someone else out there values it. It's okay—let it be. Never laugh at anyone else's dreams.

Life Lesson #9: 10 batches … and counting.

Feels like failure, doesn't it? You've baked your new recipe every way you know how and it's just not right. Don't call it a failure. Call it a challenge. With perseverance you'll get it right … or maybe you won't. Just remember, if you lose, don't lose the lesson.

Life Lesson #10: Don't mumble your thank-yous.

You've made the perfect batch of bittersweet chocolate pecan cookies. Your friends go crazy with compliments. It's okay. Enjoy the moment. But remember that pleasure lives not only in the receiving, but also in the giving. Accept compliments with humility and appreciation.

So that's it. My simple life lessons. Oh, and by the way, we never conquered the dark chocolate/white chocolate swirl issue. With great flavor, but an unappetizing appearance, we were never able to add it to our retail holiday collection. But to this day my boys (actually young men) and Solomon (my boyfriend) love it. So I guess I could say one woman's reject is another person's treasure. (LIFE LESSON #11!)

Ask Penny

Penny Answers Your Baking Questions

q I never seem to get my cookies a consistent size. What do you use to scoop the cookie dough?

a If you've mixed the dough properly it should be easy to get uniform cookies using food scoops. They are used in restaurants for portion control, but we use them (as most bakeries do) to create beautiful, uniform cookies. From tiny to huge, they're available at any good kitchen or restaurant supply store.

q Can't I just grind my own nuts instead of using nut meal?

a Nut meals are a commercial product ground from whole nuts and are a little grittier and oilier than most nut flours. You can indeed make your own nut meal in a food processor fitted with the steel blade. Just watch it carefully because it is hard to keep the nut meal from turning into nut butter. It may help to freeze the nuts before grinding and to use the pulse setting on the food processor. It also helps to add a little of the sugar in the recipe to the nuts to absorb some of the oils. By the way, if you have any left over, save it in your freezer.

q Does it make a difference what brand of flour, sugar, butter, etc., I use? Are generic and store brands just as good?

a In most cookie recipes it doesn't make any difference. That said, I have my favorites. Cookie baking is fairly forgiving; store brands usually work out just fine. However, I do not compromise on quality. I love using real, whole ingredients, and have my favorite brands of chocolate, extracts, and flavored oils. Watch those substitutions, however. Expect very different results if you substitute margarine for butter or cake flour for all-purpose flour.

q Why do some recipes call for dark brown sugar and others light brown? Is there a difference?

a This whole brown sugar thing can sound very mysterious. It isn't. Whether light or dark, brown sugar is simply white granulated sugar with the addition of syrup (usually molasses). Dark brown sugar has a mild molasses added, and light brown sugar has milder, lighter syrup. In most (if not all) recipes, they can be used interchangeably. Because of the addition of syrup, all brown sugars are moist and need to be stored and measured properly. Store the sugar in an airtight container at room temperature. If you leave the sugar out it will become very hard. You can soften the sugar again by putting it in a re-sealable plastic bag with a dampened paper towel or a slice of apple for several hours.

q My cookies spread too much. What did I do wrong?

a Sometimes it's the fault of the recipe and sometimes, as much as I hate to say it, it's your mixing style. If all the cookies from one batch of dough are giving you too much spread, the recipe may be fat heavy. Reduce the amount of fat by a couple of tablespoons and that should reduce the spread. However, you may be suffering from another problem. If you're getting mixed results from the same batch of dough—some have too much spread and others are puffy—you can't blame the recipe. In this case, the dough has not been mixed correctly. Cookies are not as delicate as cakes, but mixing still plays an important role. Be sure when you mix cookie dough that you thoroughly incorporate the creamed mixture with the flour and baking powder. Hopefully these tips will solve the spread problem.

q What is the best way to store cookies? What is the best way to store brownies?

a In general, cookies and brownies store beautifully. There are some differences in types of cookies and brownies, so let's answer this with a little list.

• Casual Cookies: (i.e., chocolate chip, etc.) Casual cookies are what's called "short shelf-life" cookies. By definition they are best eaten fresh from the oven or over a couple of days. For this short storage, just put them in a covered tin and store without refrigeration. You can, however, store the dough for casual cookies in the freezer. Just put the finished dough in protective plastic wrap or zipper-type plastic bags. Freeze for up to six weeks. You can freeze baked casual cookies, but they're never as good as fresh baked cookies. I would never recommend putting baked casual cookies in the refrigerator. The refrigerator pulls moisture from baked goods and reduces what little shelf life these cookies have. So for longer storage, use the freezer.

• Decorated Cookies: Fully decorated cookies using tinted royal icing or glaze should never be refrigerated or frozen. These cookies will be fine stored in a covered tin or plastic container. Penny's Roll And Cut recipe should give you a nice long shelf life (60 days) if they have been covered with frosting and stored properly. If you must freeze these cookies, do it before you decorate them. Freezing the cookies after decorating will affect the icing and the tints when you bring the cookies back to room temperature.

• Most Brownies: By their very nature, brownies have a longer shelf life than casual cookies. They will stay fresh for days in a covered tin or plastic container. You can also extend their freshness by cutting the brownies and wrapping the individual pieces in plastic wrap. Freeze well-covered brownies for up to six weeks.

q Why do you use shortening instead of butter in some of your recipes?

a Sometimes it's about taste, and sometimes it's about how it bakes. Generally speaking I use butter because I love the taste and texture of butter cookies. But for some cookies I really like the way vegetable shortening bakes. Take the molasses cookies. I wanted the cookies to have the smoky, deep flavor of molasses without any competition from the taste of butter. From a texture standpoint I wanted big, fat cookies with controlled spread. So I chose shortening as the fat in these cookies. By the way, we almost never use margarine in any cookie recipe. The water content of margarine varies from brand to brand, thus producing varying results, some disastrous. Never use "soft" margarine for baking. Stick with shortening or butter. If you're really in the mood for cookie baking and don't have enough butter in the house, make up the fat requirement with shortening. Your finished cookies will be just fine.

q What's the difference between baking soda and baking powder? Are they interchangeable?

a Baking powder and baking soda are the two most common leavening agents in cookies. Baking soda is simply bicarbonate of soda, while baking powder is a combination of bicarbonate of soda plus cream of tartar. Baking soda neutralizes the acidity of the dough. Baking powder already contains its own acid (cream of tartar) and will not reduce the acidity of the dough. You'll notice that high-acid recipes (for instance, Molasses Cookies)

will call for baking soda while low-acid recipes (Roll and Cut Cookies) will call for baking powder. Remember, baking is a science. Moral of this little chemistry lesson: This is not the place to experiment—use what the recipe calls for!

q Does it matter what size eggs I use? Should they be at room temperature or can they be straight from the refrigerator?

a Remember, baking is science. It's all about putting specific ingredients together, exposing them to heat for a specified amount of time and, voilà, you have heaven in your hand! So yes, egg size does make a difference. Eggs add leavening, texture, tenderness, and structure. Most recipes have been scaled and then translated to cup/tablespoon measurements for home use. So when a recipe calls for large eggs it's the liquid volume that matters here. Best to use what the recipe calls for. Also, it's best to use all ingredients at the same temperature—the dough will go together better. However, I've never experienced failure because the eggs were straight from the refrigerator.

q Does it matter if you use a liquid measuring cup to measure dry ingredients?

a It's all about accuracy. Dry cup measures are made specifically to bring the dry ingredient right up to the lip of the measuring cup for a most accurate measure without scaling. Liquid cups for home use are usually 2- or 4-cup measures. Place the cup on the counter and pour the liquid in the cup, looking at it from eye level to be assured of accuracy. In a

pinch, if I had to, I'd use a dry measure to measure liquid, but not the other way around.

q When a recipe does not specify, should I sift my flour?

a For cookies, I don't usually sift flour. The purpose of sifting flour is to aerate or lighten the flour, and to remove any little lumps that have settled or formed. In cookies, using the "scoop and sweep" dry measuring method is usually sufficient. However, if you're concerned about thoroughly mixing the leavening into the flour, or have seen mysterious dark streaks in your finished baked goods (poorly incorporated baking powder or soda), you may want to sift the flour with the leavening. If you want to be extra careful, it wouldn't hurt to give the dry ingredients another quick stir with a wooden spoon after sifting.

q My cookies aren't browning. What did I do wrong?

a Are they supposed to brown? Generally speaking, the amount of sugar in the recipe controls the amount of browning. Lots of cookies are beautifully baked with just the slightest amount of browning. I usually say the bottom of the finished cookies should be dark blond and the tops light blond. Use your finger, instead of the color, to determine if the cookies have finished baking. If the cookies are to have a cake-like consistency (the roll and cut cookies, for example) then the surface of the hot cookies should be firm to the touch. Chewy cookies will have a brownie-like feel—set along the outside edge, soft in the middle.

q What's the advantage of using parchment paper?

a I like to bake cookies with some type of pan liner. Because of the ingredients, cookies have a tendency to naturally stick to the pan. Using a pan-release spray or some type of fat directly on the cookie sheet usually results in "fringing" along the edges. Not only that, but fat on cookie sheets will usually burn and give the cookie bottoms an undesirable dark color and an awful taste (have you ever tasted burned chocolate?). Parchment paper protects your cookie sheets, gives you a nice tasty cookie, and can be used over and over again. Silicone mats are beyond wonderful (but expensive) for cookie baking.

Index to Recipes

Black Magic/White Diamonds 16

Chocolate Chip Indulgence 18

Ginger Brownies 20

Cowboy Cookies .22

Razza Ma Taz 38

River City Apricot 40

Chubbie Chunky .42

Peanut Butter Obsession 44

Snickerdoodles 66

Molasses Cookies .68

Grandmother Lewis' Tea Cakes 70

Butterscotch Chews 72

All-American Brownies 90

Oatmeal Fudge Bars 92

Wanda's Tea Cakes 94

Reba's Oatmeal Raisin Cookies 96

Peppermint Penny 118

Fruit and Nut Cups 120

Penny's Roll and Cut Recipe 122

Share Your Story

Dear Penny and Kathy, here's my cookie story:

Mail it to Cookie Stories, P.O. Box 10628, Austin, Texas 78766, and THANKS!

About the Authors

At eight years old, Penny made her first batch of cookies. By the time she was 14 years old, she knew she wanted to be a baker when she grew up. And except for her minor detour to go to college and the 10-year stint as an advertising copywriter, Penny has spent her life making cookies, teaching cookie classes, writing about cookies, and passionately building her popular 15-year-old company, Penny's Pastries. Currently, she continues her cookie crusade through creating new cookie concepts, public speaking, and teaching. *Cookie Stories* is her first book.

Since the first whiff of Snickerdoodles baking in her mom's oven, Kathy has been a lover of fresh-baked cookies. She uses every opportunity available—from cookie gift baskets for friends to emergency cookie runs in support of her busy co-workers—to share her love of cookies. With more than 16 years in a variety of corporate roles, most recently in high tech, Kathy is a communications and human resources expert. *Cookie Stories* is her first book.